SARA DANGERFIELD

LEADING SPIRITUAL HOARDERS

CREATING A CULTURE OF
DISCIPLES WHO **MAKE DISCIPLES**

©2025 by Sara Dangerfield
Published by hope*books
2217 Matthews Township Pkwy
Suite D302
Matthews, NC 28105
www.hopebooks.com

hope*books is a division of hope*media

Printed in the United States of America

First paperback edition.
Paperback ISBN: 979-8-89185-212-9
Hardcover ISBN: 979-8-89185-157-3
Ebook ISBN: 979-8-89185-158-0
Library of Congress Number: 2025930642

Unless otherwise indicated, all Scripture quotations are taken from the Holy Bible, New Living Translation, copyright © 1996, 2004, 2015 by Tyndale House Foundation. Used by permission of Tyndale House Publishers, Carol Stream, Illinois 60188. All rights reserved.

Scripture quotations are from The ESV® Bible (The Holy Bible, English Standard Version®), © 2001 by Crossway, a publishing ministry of Good News Publishers. Used by permission. All rights reserved.

hope*books
hopebooks.com
Because the world needs your hope-filled
words now more than ever

"In a world that's constantly shifting, Sara has captured the essential principles for making disciples in a culture overwhelmed by distractions. With clarity and insight, Sara reminds us of the liberating truth that "we can't take stuff with us," urging us to live with an eternal perspective. I highly recommend this book to anyone longing to experience the heartbeat of God in a fresh and powerful way."

—Dr. Douglas M. Graham
Interim President
North Central University, MN

"In *Leading Spiritual Hoarders*, Sara delivers a passionate and practical guide to breaking free from spiritual complacency and embracing the call to make disciples. With a blend of deeply personal stories, biblical insight, and actionable steps, Sara equips leaders to move beyond the walls of their churches and step into the lives of their communities. Her vulnerability, wisdom, and encouragement make this a must-read for anyone ready to lead others into transformative, missional living."

—Terry Parkman
Founder of Next Generation Leader
Global Co-Chair for Empowered21 NextGen

"In *Leading Spiritual Hoarders*, Sara Dangerfield offers a compelling call to action for church leaders to prioritize discipleship and lead by example. Sara's stories, combined with biblical narratives, create a vision for a multiplying church where every member is empowered to share their faith. This is a resource for leaders seeking to create a culture that embraces disciple-making and unleashing believers to make a kingdom impact in their communities."

—Scott Wilson
President of Ready Set Grow

"In *Leading Spiritual Hoarders*, Sara breaks down how a culture of spiritual hoarding causes us to miss out on the vibrancy of multiplication Jesus had in mind when he redeemed us and gave us new life. Through her practical examples, prepare to be challenged and changed - and don't be surprised at the unexpected opportunities you'll have to give His love away!"

—Dr. Jodi Detrick
Coach, Mentor, Speaker
Author of The Settled Soul and
The Jesus-Hearted Woman
Former Columnist for the Seattle Times

For every pastor, director, and lay leader in the church. Your life as a follower of Jesus will always have more impact than your title.

ACKNOWLEDGMENTS

To my husband, Dan. You are more than my biggest supporter. You are a man who lives out the very message of this book. I'm honored to be your wife.

To my kids, Anna, Ethan, & Caleb. Thanks for putting up with my late night writing sessions, and constant dinner conversations. I owe you a Strawberry Dr. Pepper.

To our ministry staff. You are the epitome of Kingdom Builders. To lead you, and to lead the church with you, is literally the best job in the world.

To our Journey Church family. Whoever says small midwest towns can't have a huge impact haven't met you. Your choice to reflect Jesus in our communities is making the greatest impact of all.

CONTENTS

INTRODUCTION

Serving in ministry has both its joys and its pains. It's a constant roller coaster as you celebrate the greatest of wins and grieve the most painful losses—sometimes all within one day. For those who serve as a lead pastor, staff pastor, or even as a leader in a parachurch ministry, you experience this wild roller coaster as you lead the children, students, and families within your church and community. You attend the basketball games, go to the neighborhood barbecues, do the home visits, and assist with the funerals. You grow to deeply love the people you serve as you hear their stories and walk through life with them.

My husband and I served as kids pastors for 15 years. It was our pleasure to lead families, helping them take steps toward Jesus together as a family. We learned ministry can often feel like an overly weighted blanket, where if we don't allow our head to peek out from underneath its weight, we may suffocate. Choosing to lead without keeping our eyes on Jesus will not only smother us, it will lead us down roads we don't want to find ourselves. Despite the weight, God allows us to see in our minds what could be in the lives of the people we love and serve. Living as staff pastors, we knew there was a weight to ministry. We also knew there was a different kind of weight our lead pastor carried compared to our own. It wasn't necessarily harder, nor less enjoyable; it was just... different. I had no idea how heavy that different weight could get.

Before we became lead pastors, our current church had begun updating the interior of our building. After working there for about a year, we decided to continue with the remodel. We wanted to provide a safer place for our children so families would feel comfortable bringing their children to their classes. Our church had hired former children's pastors as their lead pastors–kids and families would always be a priority. In the day and age we live, taking as many safety precautions as possible for the sake of our kiddos was important to us. In addition to this, we also believed that a welcoming environment, in both our kids' wing and the rest of our building, created a safe space for newcomers who were maybe already a little hesitant about coming to church.

Excited to build some momentum as we discussed the remodel, my husband Dan opened up our annual business meeting that year by sharing a short message on the story we read in Matthew 9. After Jesus called Matthew to follow Him, He and the disciples went to Matthew's house for dinner. The Pharisees were appalled by this gesture, knowing Matthew's reputation. Jesus proceeded to tell the religious leaders how He did not come for the righteous but for those who know they are sinners. Through this new construction project, we wanted to model Jesus. The majority of people who walk through our doors would be considered the righteous in this story. For years, our church had been reaching this demographic, but we wanted to also reach those who know they are sinners. Through new coats of paint, new rooms, and even a new roof, we wanted to remind our people of the importance of making a visitor feel both safe and welcome. We would never deviate from the things that mattered most–truth, Scripture, and sound doctrine–but we would be willing to change methods to reach a part of the community our church hadn't been able to reach yet. As my husband cast the vision for the project, sharing his heart of wanting to see young families in our city come to know Christ, something began to stir in the room. That is... until Dan opened the floor for discussion. I was not prepared for what was about to happen, nor did I ever imagine I would hear such words spoken all my life. A man stood up and angrily declared, "Since when do we care more about the people out there," he pointed to outside of the building, "than we do about the people in here?!"

I was dumbfounded. Did he not just hear the purpose for the changes? Shouldn't we do all we can, outside of sin, to reach others with the Gospel? I sat there, stunned. I asked myself, "What did we get ourselves into?"

Over the next few years, I had many weighted blanket moments. Hearing the whispers in the hallways, watching as people verbally attacked our pastoral staff, and being told we were working on building our own kingdom rather than God's, we saw how the fear of losing control, along with a desire for preferences over truth, clouded the minds of well-intentioned Christians. Instead of welcoming messy, but curious, guests into the doors of the church, they judged their lifestyles and lack of faith. Instead of allowing ourselves to be suffocated by the weight, Dan and I kept our eyes on Jesus. We asked Him to help us see what He sees when it comes to our church and our community. We refused to be intimidated by the enemy's tactics to keep this church from thriving–people's eternities were in the balance. Thankfully, our church is in a much better place now.

In the pages of *Leading Spiritual Hoarders*, I invite you to peek your head out from the weight of your role as a leader. It is not my desire to state what you've done wrong and what I've done right. Instead, I want to come alongside you as I share stories of what I've learned over the years, how we've seen God transform our church, and how together we can keep moving forward. God commissioned his followers to go and make disciples and "Teach these new disciples to obey all the commands..." he has given us (Matthew 28:20).

We will look at the condition of the church and of our own hearts, asking God to help us see the church the way He sees us. We will be honest with ourselves and with the Holy Spirit as we discover what God has in store for our churches. And we will dream of what could be. God has placed you as a leader in your church, friend. It is by no mistake you are there, and it is by no mistake you opened this book. God wants to use you and the influence He has given you to breathe new life into your congregation-life that produces great fruit. It's not about butts in the seats, it's about souls in the kingdom.

I'm not an expert. I'm from a little ol' town in the Midwest who doesn't have much influence in the church world. But I've learned what it looks like to walk in obedience, to stare the enemy down and say, "Try as you may, you will not stop me from fulfilling the one thing God has asked me to do: make disciples." My desire for you is through this book, you find new rhythms that will not only help your church grow, but will help you flourish as a follower of Jesus.

CHAPTER ONE

LETTING DREAMS DIE

"Now all glory to God, who is able, through His
mighty power at work within us, to accomplish in-
finitely more than we might ask or think."
—*Ephesians 3:20*

I was a Middle Eastern girl who was raised in a Scan-
dinavian world. Raised in central Minnesota in the
90's, I wasn't exactly living in the most colorful area
of the nation at the time. Surrounded by blue eyes and
blonde hair, I never felt like I quite fit in. Even though my
mother was raised on a farm in the same town, my Middle Eastern-ness was pretty evident with my dark brown
hair, brown eyes, and olive skin. Besides that, my roots
ran deep when it came to my love of ethnic food, art,
and music. It's hard to grow up more "cultured" than your
classmates without having an increased curiosity for the
globe. My heart for the nations grew quickly in those early years as I consumed books and magazines highlighting
different areas of the world. Whether it was a tribe in the
Amazon, a village in East Africa, or a hidden community
in the Pacific Islands, I began to dream of living in foreign

lands as I shared Jesus with the locals. This dream carried on for years until one day, it all came crashing down.

We had been serving as children's pastors, proudly proclaiming we were KidMin lifers. We loved the younger generation and believed God wanted to use them for so much more than most adults gave them credit for. However, fourteen years in, we began to feel a stirring. We didn't know exactly what God was up to, but we knew it would be something brand new. Secretly, I hoped God was going to call us to work with children overseas. There were so many opportunities to reach children all around the world, especially in countries like the Philippines and Burundi.

We patiently waited to see what God would bring to the surface. We prayed. We anticipated. We continued to serve. Then, one day, a friend contacted us and asked if we had ever considered lead pastoring. There was a church a few hours down the road from us that needed a pastor, and he felt my husband Dan was the man for the job. We had no interest in being lead pastors, but as a few weeks went by, my husband couldn't shake the conversation with our friend. Getting into bed one night, he looked at me and said, "I can't get the neighboring church out of my head. I think we need to at least explore it and see what God does." Coldly, I gave him a dead stare, rolled over, and went to bed. No way! I didn't want to be a lead pastor's wife. This was not the plan. It was not the dream—the dream I'd had since childhood. To say I was upset would've been an understatement.

When I'm not in the disposition to learn, it seems as though God finds my sour mood to be a perfect opportunity to teach me a thing or two. I'm not sure if you deal with it or not, but I can be ranting and raving about how mad or upset I am over something, then all of a sudden, I can physically feel Him sitting in the room. I envision Him sitting in the corner recliner, with the look of a father who has a readied lesson in his pocket, waiting patiently for me to finish with my rampage. Aren't you glad for God's grace, whose understanding is far beyond our own? It's important to remind ourselves how our perspective is so limited, yet God is still willing to work with us.

With my tail between my legs and not wanting to cause division, I let my husband put in a resume. I figured the church would look at these two kid pastors, laugh, think it was "cute" that we put in a resume with no experience, and then move on. Of course, that didn't happen. We walked through interviews, had tough conversations, and much to my dismay (and through more prayer than I've ever prayed before), we took the plunge and agreed to the one thing I never wanted to do. I'd like to say I joyfully walked this road, but I can't. Although God confirmed to both of us that this is where He wanted us in this new season, I wasn't thrilled.

After we moved into our new home, the kids were settled in their new schools, and we stepped into our new pastoring role, I knew it was time to have a face-to-face with God. All the changes kept me busy, but now I found myself stewing. I was indignant. I didn't get it, and I was tired of not understanding why God wouldn't let me chase after my dream. After getting the kids to school one day, with my husband at the office, I settled into our quiet home. It wasn't my proudest moment as I sat on the floor and pouted like a three-year-old. The quiet around me was deafening, and I could feel my emotions boiling inside. Ashamed of how angry I had become, and with a little trepidation, I told God how I felt. "It's not fair." "I'm not made for this job." "I don't even like adults!!" The response I received? Nothing. I felt like the prophet Jeremiah. He was sent to be a voice of truth, and even though it was a good thing–he didn't want to do it. The people he had to speak with and point out their sins were not his favored audience. Maybe this is how my teenagers feel, too, when I stare at them after a rampage. As their mom, I listen intently but say nothing... because I know nothing will make it better in the moment. God also knew nothing in the moment would've satisfied my spewing.

After letting it all out, I needed to begin preparing a sermon I'd preach a few weeks later. Being a kid's pastor was fun because we used object lessons and puppets. However, they didn't prepare me for the work ahead as I gathered a message for those who had lived longer and learned great wisdom even before I breathed my first breath. Ironically, I was writing a message of gratitude. Looking at the book of Colossians, I read Paul's account to the people on how God wanted them to clothe themselves with tenderhearted mercy, kindness, humility, gentleness, and patience. They were to clothe themselves with love and let the peace of God rule their hearts (Colossians 3:12-15). Unfortunately, my heart did not match the message I was preparing. I was angry. I was impatient and fed up with letting God's peace rule my heart. I look back now and laugh because God's timing in this lesson could not have been more perfect.

In the middle of sermon prepping, with Paul's words jumping off the page, I came to grips with how wrong I was. My pride kept me from asking questions humbly. So I closed my notebook, pushed my chair away from my desk, put my face into my hands, and cried. This time, choosing a posture of humility, I asked God for discernment. This began a cycle of grief because I began to grieve what I hoped would have been. With tears in my eyes, I looked up at my ceiling and said, "God! I don't get it. Your Word literally says you are looking for people to go to the nations. You are scanning the earth looking for people who are willing to go, and here I am–waving my arms, jumping up and down–saying, 'Pick me! Pick me!' And instead of choosing me to go, you continue to put me locally, telling me yet again to drive down the road a few hours and work in a nearby church. In a position I had no interest in serving, no less. WHY?!" After my honest rant, feeling His presence near, I heard Him whisper to the deep part of my soul, "Yes, Sara. I let your dream of going to the nations die. I let your dream die because it wasn't mine. It simply wasn't big enough." All of a sudden, I felt a wave of nausea run through me. I had gone too far. But did that stop me? Unfortunately, no.

Pushing even harder against Him (like I said, I was trying to be humble, but I was definitely a work in progress), I audibly yelled, "What's bigger than giving up everything to go overseas?! Giving up my comfort, giving up living near my family, giving up a secure income?" Let's just say it wasn't my shining moment. I didn't see a vision, but I felt the atmosphere in the room change. Almost as if He went from being seated in the comfy chair in the corner to a standing position near His throne, God brought me down as quickly as my pride attempted to bring me up. What he said next changed my life forever. He said, "Sara. Look back at the last fourteen years. Look at the students you served. How many of them are living thriving relationships with me? How many of them are serving me in a ministry capacity? How many of them are making plans to serve in a missionary role for the rest of their lives? Imagine how many more there would have been if you had been more intentional." The wind was pulled from my sails as I hung my head in humility. He didn't send me to my new city because I was being punished. He didn't send me because I'm not cut out for overseas work. Instead, He saw the gifts He gave me as useful for sending others. As He began to lay out His plan, He told me those I disciple here can do far more for the kingdom than just my little family of five. If I could multiply my heart for others to know Him, I would honor God and help grow His kingdom through others who said 'yes.' Whether it's overseas, in their workplace, or in their neighborhood, God wanted to use people right here in North Dakota to make a kingdom impact. Regrettably, I was immature as a leader and needed to continue growing in my spiritual walk to see how God wanted me to see. I was so tunnel-visioned on what the mission looked like that I missed the fact God was already using me in that capacity. **Imagine what He could do once I understood the task He had given me when it came to growing God's kingdom, allowing His dream to become my own.** Some of us go. Some of us give. Some of us send. My job was to send–to intentionally make disciples who make disciples.

Before giving me the death of dreams talk, for many years, I felt God was putting my dream on pause. I loved ministry, don't get me wrong. Serving in the local church matured my faith and grew my heart toward the very things Paul mentioned in Colossians: humility, patience, and tenderhearted mercy. There are certain things I never would've learned had I not served in the local church. I'm sure you could say the same thing. Therefore, I had to make a choice: what would I do in the waiting? As you read, I grew impatient by the minute and chose to wallow in my emotions in the waiting. Looking back, I'm reminded of how thankful I am for His grace, which I unquestionably did not deserve.

Before we continue, let me encourage you. Maybe you have felt the same way: feeling stuck where you're serving, whether as a punishment or to prove a point that you can or cannot do something. May I remind you that you have not been placed where you are because of these reasons. Rather, you are in your church because people need you there. Your time may be undetermined, but God has assigned you there for a specific reason and season. Let's celebrate and be thankful for the lives God has put in front of us to serve and influence. If you recognize you've had a bad attitude like I did, then it's time to have a heart-to-heart with Jesus. Take a few moments, with a repentant heart, to ask Him to show you the dreams He has for you and your community. You will not be disappointed.

Just as God put a pause on my dream of leading the nations to Christ, He did the same for Paul's ministry as well. You could even call it an inconvenience. During his second missionary journey, Paul wanted to travel to new places so the Gospel could be spread even further, but the Holy Spirit prevented him from going to certain regions multiple times. We don't know how this happened, but as we read in Acts 16, it's clear the Spirit prevented Paul and Silas from traveling to the provinces of both Asia and Bithynia. As he settled in for the night in Alexandria Troas, Paul had a dream. In his dream, a man from Macedonia was calling out to him, asking for help. It was just a dream, but Paul knew the dream was from the Lord. Immediately the next morning, Paul and Silas, along with their new friend Luke, headed to Macedonia as a result of the dream and what God was asking them to do. God wasn't placing a pause on Paul's ministry because of something Paul did. No, He did it so Luke could join them and be used as well. This is the same Luke we know who wrote both the Gospel of Luke and the Book of Acts. God was letting someone else do what Paul desired, making space for Luke to use his own gifts for the Kingdom of God. Luke wrote significantly more of the New Testament than any other writers, including Paul himself.

We still feel the ripples of what Luke witnessed and wrote about years ago, all because Paul picked up this new guy in Troas on their journey. Today, Luke's writings teach and guide us as we learn to follow God's leading. Paul didn't need to know why there was a pause; he just needed to say, "Yes, I will do what you lead me to do." Like Paul, I needed to do the same. As I chose to step into more of a sending role, I set aside my pride and gave others the opportunity to serve God in only ways they could.

Changing roles and accepting this new dream God had for me allowed me to see things from a new perspective. What I hadn't seen when working with young families were the holes in how the church as a whole functioned. I saw adults afraid of sharing their faith with others (even their own children), feeling ill-equipped, and choosing to remain silent instead of fulfilling the Great Commission God placed on them as believers. This was news to me after having worked with kids who have faith much larger than a mustard seed–it was more like the size of the ocean. Veils had been peeled from my eyes as I saw the local church in a whole new way. It was a group of people with so much untapped potential. Many knew the Lord, but they didn't know what that meant for their daily lives. The potential I saw was endless, but I honestly had no idea how to tap into it.

Maybe that's what you're feeling today. Maybe you have a deep inner yearning, believing there's got to be something more for your church. What we're doing isn't working, and we know it to be true as we watch churches in our communities continue to dwindle. Unfortunately, this isn't a new development. It happened in the New Testament, too, as church numbers rose and fell. I believe Paul was spot on when he told Timothy how the people in Ephesus had missed the whole point of being a follower of Jesus. He wanted all believers to be filled with love, having a pure heart, a clear conscience, and a genuine faith (1 Timothy 1:5-6). But people were caught up with things that didn't matter. They wanted to be known as people who had the answers so they could point out the sin in others. Like today, Paul saw the church in Ephesus had become like a club sport. As an exclusive club, people could come to them and receive instruction to better themselves. Ephesians didn't gather this knowledge to share it with others; they simply were consumers.

The American church is guilty of the same thing. Somewhere down the road, spiritual formation was taken off the body of believers and put on the building. The building became the place where people could be discipled, allowing them to essentially hoard the Gospel for themselves. Part of the problem is America's culture of individualism. Barna Research states, "56% of Christians feel their spiritual life is entirely private."[1] If

1 https://www.barna.com/research/discipleship-friendship/

they consider it private, they are definitely not sharing it with anyone else. Instead, people just bring a friend with them to church and allow someone else to do the teaching. Then they walk out the door and head to the closest restaurant, all without a word of how the message impacted them and what God spoke to them as a result of it. You and I are the someone else they defer to. As pastors and ministry leaders, we have allowed others to use us as an avenue to disciple their friends and family—something God has actually called them to do. It may not have started with us, but between the leadership of pastors before us and our continued direction, the church is not living up to its potential. I now see what God was trying to convey to me. My heart for the nations is what now motivates my heart for the American church. Look at all of its potential!

Seeing the concern for the American church, we need to ask a few questions: Are we able to shift the mindset of individualism in our churches, which is very me-centered, to a perspective of collectivism, which cares for the greater good of the church? I sure think so! Can we come alongside the people in our churches and help cultivate an environment for growth in the spiritual formation of their friends and families? Definitely. However, should we be the sole source of discipleship? Nope. When Jesus commissioned His disciples in Matthew 28 and again in Acts 1, He commissioned all believers to teach new disciples in the way of Jesus. *All.* It will take laying down dreams in order to break free from spiritual hoarding so we can step into spiritual sharing.

'Spiritual hoarders' is a strong phrase, and I understand that. Maybe the bold phrase was enough to create some curiosity, causing you to snag this book off the shelf. The expression was birthed out of frustration as I watched people act as though their lips were stapled shut, not allowing them to have faith conversations with those around them. I felt like the psalmist when they said, "I became furious with the wicked, because they reject your instructions" (Psalms 119:53). There's no doubt our post-modern world has made it more difficult to have faith conversations. As truth constantly shifts in today's culture, people don't know what kind of response they will get from others if they try to bring up Jesus. But when we choose not to share, then we are truly hoarding the Gospel for ourselves. Yes, hoarding.

Hoarding is defined as the persistent struggle of parting with possessions, regardless of their value. In fact, the idea of parting with it causes distress as people question if it's worth the risk of damaging relationships. Just like those who hoard physical items, many believe it's not worth the risk of damaging a relationship and ultimately choose their love for people over their love for their Savior. Our love for Him should result in sharing Him with others, not keeping Him to ourselves. Furthermore, similar to those with hoarding disorders, they need to be taught how to share what they've held so tightly. They need someone to walk life with them, who will step-by-step show them how to let go of what is precious to them so others may benefit as well.

Friends, hoarding the Gospel not only stunts our personal growth, it ultimately stunts the church's growth as well. We saw this happening when influential voices in our church declared the importance of caring for those inside the building above and beyond those who were outside of it—much like the man from the business meeting I mentioned earlier. Please know, I'm not just talking about the people in your church—I'm talking about you. **Believe it or not, pastors can be guilty of keeping the best news on this planet to themselves as well.** We can get so caught up in doing the ministry that we no longer see the person at the register in the grocery store or the young teen who wanders the neighborhood. We no longer look for ways to "Make the most of every opportunity in these evil days" (Ephesians 5:16).

My daughter was working on a history assignment in our living room one day. Her teacher was asking the students to summarize the main worldwide religions. Wanting to finish her assignment quickly, she exasperatedly asked her dad, "Why can't everyone just love Jesus?!" I peeked my head around the corner and said, "It's because so many Christians aren't telling other people about Him!" When we boil it down, what's really happening is the big 'C' church is losing ground. It's not because of a lack of flashy Sunday morning experiences, trendy pastors, and seeker-friendly services. It's because the people who sit in the seats aren't showing their friends the relevancy of the Gospel. I'd love to say there's a magic sermon you can share that will light a fire under your parishioners, but I can't. It takes a leader who is willing to fight for the Gospel and advocate for participation in the Great Commission, who can help change the culture in their church so we can work to rectify this problem. It takes ministry leaders and pastors who can humbly accept their dreams aren't as big as God's.

In the Old Testament, we read how Jacob had a dream which was forced to be laid to rest as well. After running away from family troubles, he found himself living with his uncle. Waiting for things to smooth over with his family, he let time pass by serving his uncle. During this time, he worked very hard to receive a young woman named Rachel as his wife. He fell in love with Rachel shortly after meeting her, taking in her beautiful figure and lovely face. Along with her father Laban, Jacob worked out a bride price to take Rachel as his wife. For seven years, Jacob labored and toiled over Laban's land and flocks. However, on the night of their wedding, he discovered he had been tricked by his new father-in-law. Unknowingly, Jacob entered into a marriage that evening with Rachel's sister, Leah. This was not the plan! His dream had been a life with Rachel. Continuing to pursue his dream, he worked another seven years to gain his one true love.

Jacob pursued dreams many of us have had: love, money, praise, and more. God had bigger dreams, though. He dreamt of restoration and raising up a nation of people who would be a worldwide witness of God's power and love. As well-intentioned as his dreams were,

Jacob needed to lay them down for the sake of God's plans. He found himself doing that very thing when Rachel passed away because of complications in childbirth. Jacob had to lay his beautiful wife to rest in a wilderness burial marked by a stone monument. How his heart must have ached to lose his love. In the midst of his pain, he chose not to remain at her grave; he had to move on. He had to move forward in order for God to accomplish the things He wanted to do in, and through, Jacob.

The road I took to get here wasn't an easy one. I look back and wish my eyes had been opened to my pride and selfishness, wanting to go after my own desires–all cloaked with "for the sake of Jesus." However, if it hadn't been for the seasons that led me here, I wouldn't have encountered the lessons I learned along the way. Even as a leader in ministry, I was one of those Christians who wasn't telling other people about Him unless I was hidden behind my title of pastor. Thank God for His patience as He slowly pulled one layer at a time off my blinded eyes as I laid down my dreams.

I may not have become a missionary in a foreign land (who knows, maybe one day I will!), but it was a result of my plans shifting from being mine to being His; the death of one dream gave birth to another. I dream of the 56% feeling empowered and emboldened to share their faith. I dream of pre-believers being discipled in the ways of Jesus and finding freedom in the truth of His word. Just like Jacob, I dream of the next generation being raised as believers who are assured in their walk with God and can confidently share the Gospel message with their friends.

I dream of churches busting at the seams because the building cannot contain the people who are hungry to hear the word of God. Whether it's in Brazil or North Dakota, I dream of people knowing Him.

So here we are: a group of leaders and pastors who want to see the church grow. It's about allowing God to birth new dreams in us. It's about being willing to see leadership from a new perspective. It's about digging our heels in, doing hard work, and seeing fruit because of it.

The potential is endless with God's people. God wanted to use my life as an example to help draw out the possibilities of those who attend my church. He asked me to lead the way in what it looked like to disciple others. So this is my story. But I must warn you, if you're not interested in stirring the waters a little and embarking on what could be a life-changing journey, then I would suggest you stick this book right back on the shelf. Let it collect dust or even give it away. Reading it will not leave you the same. Some of the principles are simple, but others–when you look deep into your very soul–will challenge you like no other.

Reflection Questions:

- When you first stepped into ministry, what were some of your dreams?

- Do you consider your faith to be private? Why or why not?

- Are there dreams God is asking you to lay down? If so, what is it?

CHAPTER TWO

CULTIVATING A HEALTHY ENVIRONMENT

"I have come to call not those who think they are righteous, but those who know they are sinners and need to repent." —Luke 5:32

My sister is a flower farmer right here in the heart of North Dakota. Every day she straps on her overalls and throws on her boots as she heads outside for her flower plots. Inspiring others with her videos and photos on social media, she has made her own corner of the world a more colorful place. Her green thumb started by watching our mother care for the few potted plants she had on our patio while we were growing up. As an adult, my sister began to explore gardening during a very hard season of her life, hoping it would spark some life inside her weary soul. Watching her thrive today and turning her hobby into a business makes me well up with pride. It's unfortunate that while she has the greenest thumb of anyone I know, the potted plants she gives me prove I did not get the same gardening genes. While her land is filled with blooms of intricate petals and brilliant colors, I can't even keep a plant from being suffocated by weeds before it reveals its beauty.

Her road is less traveled in the upper Midwest. She has had to push through the challenges of growing both delicate and hardy flowers in some of the harshest conditions. Visiting her farm always brings a smile to my face. Each season brings something to the table for her promising business. Every Christmas, I find her divulging in all things plants and flower farming. From magazines to books and blogs, she maps out her new spaces before winter has even hit its stride. In the spring, my nephew will show me where his vegetable garden will be while his mom will lift the tarps off her low tunnels to show what is already blossoming underneath. With the summer heat, she has a chance to show off all her hard work as we walk through rows and rows of plants. There's always something new to explore, smell, and snap photos of as she prepares for businesses and brides who want locally sourced blooms for their events. Driven to succeed, she loves growing flowers that should not be able to thrive in our colder environment–and she's doing just that.

A gardener has one job: to cultivate an environment where plants can grow. From the soil to the sunshine, my sister does what she can to help produce a colorful crop. Over time, she's had to adapt as she learns what helps or hinders her plants. From snow run-off in the spring to high winds and grasshoppers in the summer, she's adjusted with each crop so she can have a larger yield than the year before. The abundant sunshine North Dakota brings, along with high-producing pollinators, make for an incredible bloom harvest–if the farmer knows what they're doing. She doesn't grow delphinium, dahlias, and ranunculus in our unpredictable NoDak weather just for the heck of it. She grows them so she can both enjoy them and share them. However, she is unable to do that if she first doesn't cultivate a healthy environment.

As pastors and leaders, it is imperative we cultivate a healthy environment within our churches. When the people we've been entrusted with get excited to grow in their relationship with God and share the message of the Gospel with others, the church is alive! It is thriving, filled with people who are abundant in faith and flourishing in their understanding of what a Christ-follower looks like. Nevertheless, much of the American church today is apathetic, showing a lack of interest or concern in growing in these areas.

Scripture addresses the spirit of apathy in a letter Jesus wrote to the Laodiceans in Revelation. The congregation in Laodicea was dominated by Jewish believers, and the letter was written a couple of generations after the church had been founded. Jesus told them, "I know all the things you do, that you are neither hot nor cold. I wish that you were one or the other! But since you are like lukewarm water, neither hot nor cold, I will spit you out of my mouth!" (Revelation 3:15-16).

We often interpret the passage of being hot or cold, and not being a lukewarm believer, by saying we shouldn't be wishy-washy in our faith. This can certainly be one application, but discovering its more accurate meaning brings an even greater understanding of how apathy can hurt the church. Laodicea did not have a sustainable water source during the Roman Empire. In fact, the rulers and emperors of the day prided themselves on being able to build cities where cities should not have been because of resource availability. Laodicea was a product of their willingness to take on a challenge. They created a seven-mile aqueduct system just to be sure the people had access to water; it wasn't an easy system. The water had such high amounts of calcium in it that hard deposits would encase the pipes, choking the water flow. In addition to this struggle, the water could not be used if it wasn't at the right temperature.

The aqueducts came from two different places. North of the valley, they were able to get hot water for therapeutic purposes. From the south, they could get cold, drinkable water. It was a complicated method, yet fascinating they could make it work without modern-day technology. A beautiful parallel is hidden within this letter Jesus wrote to the Laodiceans. If the hot water from the north didn't stay hot, it could no longer be used for therapy. In addition, if the water from the south did not reach the people at the adequate temperature, it was no longer drinkable and, therefore, useless. It would become tepid, taste nasty, and would lose all its natural properties. No one in their right mind would drink it.

I had an opportunity to visit Laodicea in 2022, and it was massive! The ruins of the city were first discovered in 2002, which is an incredibly new discovery in archaeological terms. While there, guests are given the opportunity to experience a Roman bath. I love to take a good long bath–with some chocolates and a good book, of course–but this was an entirely different venture. I'm not the most adventurous person in the world, but the friend I was traveling with definitely was. Putting my best foot forward, I gave it a shot and had quite the encounter. Before entering the pool, we were required to rinse in the shower, wear a cloth swim cap graciously given to us by the establishment, and slowly step into a hot pool that was so murky that it was impossible to see through the water. It was hot–taking me a good five minutes to get settled in the water! Looking around at the group I traveled with, I found myself laughing hysterically. We looked like we'd fit in an animated film with the brightly colored cloth caps on our heads instead of an adventurous lot. This is what you do when you travel to exotic places, though, right? From this hot pool, we moved to an even hotter one. Measured at 115 degrees Fahrenheit, I struggled getting in the water past my ankles. We were supposed to immerse ourselves up to our shoulders in the sea of steam, but this naturally hot box of a girl couldn't handle the temperature. Instead, I gladly sat on the edge of the rocky steps while dipping my toes in the scalding water. Afterward, we rinsed in ice-cold water and, lastly, were sent to a cold pool. We were told going from pool to pool helped stimulate the circulatory system in the body, improve the respiratory system, and reduce tension. People would cycle from hot to hotter to cold and over again until they reached an almost euphoric state. While I only encountered red toes and a cold nose, it was an experience I'll never forget.

The hottest of hot water came from a natural hot spring. If it wasn't hot after traveling through the aqueducts, it was considered useless. Jesus was using this as a lesson. Just like water that is neither hot nor cold loses its usefulness, having no value or purpose, so had the church in Laodicea. Becoming lukewarm, the church had lost its witness because it had become complacent and apathetic. The city literally saw no threat in the church- no threat to the Roman Empire and no threat to the evil happening all around them.

We've often misinterpreted this Scripture, thinking we need to be hot and on fire for Jesus. When really, Jesus is just saying, "**Be the temperature I created you to be**. You have a purpose, and I want you to live in a way where you can do the things I've called you to do."

Throughout the entirety of the letter, Jesus was calling them out for their apathy, indifference, and spiritual lukewarmness. He doesn't tell them this because He is punishing them; He is warning them. He reassures them His rebuke is completely out of love but tells them it's time to turn from their current state. He asked them to turn away from their wishy-washy lifestyle and instead truly seek and say yes to His lordship over their lives. The believers of Laodicea knew Jesus superficially and had forsaken Him for the things of this world. He was offering them a way back into a right relationship with Him.

The problem is apathy doesn't just hurt the believer or the church. It hurts the unbeliever as well. It isn't just a "You do you, and I'll do me" situation, where we can choose to be serious about our faith whenever we want. Apathy hurts all people. It is a big reason why teens and young adults are leaving the church in droves–because they've been hurt by someone in the church who was hypocritical in behavior or because they had parents who were lukewarm. This kind of indifference hurts adults because they see their co-workers, neighbors, and friends living one way on Sunday and another Monday-Saturday; they don't see fruit from their professed faith. Apathy even hurts children because they don't see the importance, the urgency, or the purpose in following Jesus. Sadly, only a quarter of those living in the United States claim to be Evangelical.[2] This isn't saying only a quarter of our nation are Christians because many people will mark Christian on a form when prompted to. Instead, it's saying one in four Americans have an understanding of who Jesus is and the relationship He wants to have with us as his followers. Only one in four. Does this hurt your heart? It sure hurts mine. We can sit here and say our churches are fine and seem to be healthy, but if they were actually healthy, they'd reflect higher numbers, wouldn't they? If our churches were taking upon themselves the call to 'go and make disciples,' we'd see it indicated by growth.

---

2 "United States." Joshua Project, https://joshuaproject.net/countries/US. Accessed 28 June 2024.

The numbers don't lie. We know something needs to change. Whether we can put our finger on it or not, we know what we are doing isn't working. We could argue our methods aren't challenging attendees to be bold and courageous in their faith. Is it possible the culture many of our churches have is cultivating apathy? Whether it was created by generational opinions and preferences, well-intentioned leaders, or even from fear of repeating a past experience, the culture many churches have is unhealthy–and, quite frankly, unbiblical. When the American church first opened its doors, they allowed anyone in. We hear it in stories like that of a young preacher named David Wilkerson, who reached out to gang members in New York City[3]. Or in the lives of Dwight L. Moody[4] and Emma Dryer[5], who saw the need to raise new leaders in the faith to help continue the movement of reaching the lost. They were evangelistic in nature, claiming things like, "Jesus saves! Hear how He saves the lost, the brokenhearted, the hurting, and your life will never be the same!" Our own church has a history of its own active evangelism. In its early days, our church met in all kinds of locations, one of them being a beauty parlor. They would tell those in the community, "Come on in, and let God beautify you inwardly!"

3 "Teen Challenge USA History." Delmarva Teen Challenge, https://www.delmarvateenchallenge.org/tcusahistory.html. Accessed 2 July 2024.
4 "D. L. Moody." Moody Bible Institute, https://www.moody.edu/about/our-bold-legacy/d-l-moody/. Accessed 17 May 2024.
5 "Emma Dryer." Moody Bible Institute Archives, https://public-safety.moody.edu/library-home/archives/biographies/emma-dryer/. Accessed 30 June 2024.

Today, many people in our cities hear things more similar to "Clean up before you come to church." I know this to be true because I've heard it from the mouths of people in our church. They were so concerned with other people's sins, that they forgot Jesus loved them in their own struggles, too.

Is this the opinion of everyone in the four walls of our churches? No, of course not. But it can often be the loud voices. These are the voices casting judgment on the non-believer. They are also the voices who threaten the pastor to withhold finances or involvement unless things are done in a manner they believe it should be done. Again, how this culture came about can vary as much as the colors in the sky during a sunrise. We can't change the past and the experiences people have had, but we can begin to intentionally work the ground toward changing the culture in our churches today. The indifference we see when it comes to faith and a relationship with Jesus puts people's eternities in the balance. If we truly love people, wouldn't we want to show them the best example of Jesus we can show them... in us? In order to do this, we must take the blinders off our eyes and look at our church for what it truly is. This is what Dan and I had to do when first coming to our church. Our blinders came abruptly off during that meeting years ago, but for others, it may be gradual as you pray for your eyes to see and your ears to hear. Each of us has to evaluate where we are so we know where we want to go–how we want to move forward in creating a culture within our churches of disciples who make disciples.

I've learned there are four major indicators we can look at to help us accurately assess our church's condition. Every church is different, as their styles reflect their communities, and that's okay. In fact, it's good. We should be relatable to those who live life near us. When the culture looks less like Jesus, though, and more like the world, we have problems. As we begin to cultivate a healthy culture in our churches, we begin to see a multiplying culture unfold.

The first indicator we see in a multiplying church is when its attendees are *energized by their faith*. Just like my sister's plants, capturing energy from the sun in order to grow, our people will grow when their faith is activated. Paul says to let our roots grow down deep and allow our lives to be built on Christ alone. Our faith will strengthen as we make truth our foundation (Colossians 2:7). Faith is built, grows, and runs deep when we make Christ our foundation. When He becomes our cornerstone, we are eager to thrive in the purpose God has for us. If we aren't showing fruit of that, then our faith is dead, and so are our churches. A healthy church is alive and growing!

Growth can happen in many ways. For example, when we stepped over the threshold of our kindergarten classrooms, we were hungry to learn. Before any of us were greeted by our enthusiastic teachers, we may have already started the fundamentals of tying our shoes, how to zip our own jackets, and sharing our crayons and classroom toys. These patient instructors taught us lessons in life and schooling in a place of discovery. The greatest of these lessons was the notorious ABCs. Looking both familiar and peculiar, the shapes of these newfound letters would open doors of new possibilities. Learning the alphabet, however, wouldn't immediately turn us into accomplished chapter book readers. Knowing the basics was only a stepping stone to a world filled with stories for us to devour.

Faith grows by reading God's Word. When a person only gets their dose of Scripture one day a week by attending local church services, how do we anticipate them gaining wisdom, finding their identity in Christ, and learning what God expects of them as His follower? Unfortunately, just like our kindergarten teachers, we can't make people follow our instructions. We know reading the Bible will open doors of new possibilities, but we can't force people to open it up and read it. **What we can do, however, is cultivate an environment that sets them up to win if they're hungry and willing to learn.**

Serving as kids pastors for as long as we did, Dan and I dealt with all kinds of situations as we tried to inspire children to make their faith their own–not depending on their parents' faith in order to call themselves a Christian. Years ago, one of our students named Carter would walk into my fifth grade Sunday School class nearly every Sunday with a huge grin on his face. He would saunter in, find his seat, and wait for the perfect moment to set us all up for a good laugh. He was smart. He didn't always make the wisest of choices, but he had a good head on his shoulders for only being ten years old. Carter was eager to learn, but he rarely dug for answers as we discussed stories from the Pentateuch all the way to the Gospels. I would go home in the afternoons frustrated because I knew he was a sponge waiting to soak up all he could. Yet his actions didn't prove what I knew to be true. I later discovered while this class was fun, filled with games and stories, I wasn't allowing the students to discover answers for themselves. They were simply regurgitating what they'd been told, whether by me or even their parents, considering their answers to be 'good enough' to get by. I wasn't creating an environment where learning was being cultivated. Their knowledge was just transplanted, with nothing to encourage further growth. When Carter hit High School, he had a leader who challenged him and pushed him toward growth, beginning a journey of taking his faith seriously. He was not only encouraged to study the Word on his own, he was held accountable for how he chose to live according to the words we read on a regular basis. Thanks to that leader and others like him, Carter is now pastoring his own congregation as he charges others to make their Christian walk a daily lifestyle.

Secondly, when a church holds an *outward mindset*, it is more likely to have a multiplying culture. The body consists of a collaboration of hearts in each person attending the church, and it takes self-awareness to know the condition of those hearts. This is a hot topic in church leadership because we never want to have an inward mindset, right? As it should be. But I want to take a slightly different angle with this, if you don't mind.

During my early years, I remember the church I attended providing many activities for our community. As we entertained others with Christmas musicals and evangelistic productions, we were indirectly telling our community, "Come and see." Are these bad things? No way. I know many people who've come to know Christ because of activities just like these. I don't remember, however, much of what we did for our community that had us 'go and do.' Maybe we did, and those memories are lost to me now. Even so, it's been the same in churches Dan and I have served in over the years. Rarely do I remember actually going out into our community and meeting people in their corner of the world. I know of churches who have handed out water at holiday parades or provided food after community events. Instead of waiting for someone to walk in their doors, they have chosen to walk their city's streets. It's cliché, but if I knew someone was going to get hit by a bus, I wouldn't sit in my car and honk at them. I'd run out of my vehicle and pull them to safety. We do this by going to those in our community, actively living as the hands and feet of Jesus.

It wasn't until we moved to our current church that I participated in a church-wide 'go and do' event. Our local university was preparing for homecoming, and a group of people in our church saw a perfect opportunity to serve, with the purpose of telling the community we love them. Seeing the need for more tailgating food, they asked permission from the school to serve free burgers and hot dogs to add to the festivities. Hesitantly, the school agreed. Throwing on any university gear we had, people in our church joyfully served hot dogs and burgers to students, parents, and faculty. Many, including the university's president, paused with a plate of food in their hand and asked, "Why are you willing to give this to us for free? You could make so much money doing this!" Each time, we responded with, "Because Jesus loves you, and so do we."

As we 'go and do,' it becomes clear that churches with an outward mindset have a heart for the lost. It isn't just the few who actively pray and seek ways to reach them; it's the general body. To further illustrate, many of us do a 'come and see' event every summer: Vacation Bible School. However, we can quickly turn this into a 'go and do' event. A summer VBS isn't just so children in the community can have a safe place to be for the week and to hear about Jesus. It provides a unique opportunity for the church to build a relationship with families in their neighborhood. The church can knock on doors to share about their event, learn the names of their neighbors, and take the time to hear their stories. We don't have to just ask them to come to our four walls; we can go to theirs as well. The church exists so others may hear, and those others may be right in our own neighborhoods. I'm not saying you should go feed your local students or put on a VBS, but what I am saying is it's important we evaluate what our churches are doing. Do we have a balanced model that includes both 'come and see' with 'go and do,' or are we stuck like so many other ministries have been for a long time?

Actively seeking to find what God wants is yet another indicator of a healthy, multiplying culture. When I was a child, I was faced with a decision. At ten years old, I received a gift package in the mail from my grandparents. As Muslims, they became concerned for my spiritual condition as they saw me leaning toward, and growing in, my mother's Christian faith. In the package were books about their religion, the history behind their faith, and how they did rituals before prayer. It was a well-intentioned gift, but it put my childhood self in quite the predicament. Would I please my mom, or would I please my grandparents? I quickly learned the valuable lesson of pleasing God over pleasing people. I knew what this would cost me, no matter which route I chose. But if I was willing to walk in obedience to God, I would be rewarded. My relationship with my grandparents left in disrepair, I now look back and can resonate with the psalmist when he said, "How kind the Lord is! How good he is. So merciful, this God of ours! The Lord protects those of childlike faith; I was facing death, and he saved me" (Psalm 116:5-6). Although it hurts to be estranged from family, pleasing my Heavenly Father far surpasses any other desire I have.

Paul said it so eloquently when he told the Galatians if pleasing people were his goal, he would not be Christ's servant (Galatians 1:10). Churches who count the cost and are willing to lay down whatever it is the Lord asks them to surrender will not only be Christ's servants, they will be rewarded with a healthy culture. This may mean making decisions where not everyone agrees. Discerning the difference between foundational truths and superfluous preferences is part of our role as a leader. We may lose people or even finances, but if our goal is to be obedient and to reach the lost, then the cost is worth it. How do you make decisions for your church or ministry? Is it based on what other churches down the road are doing, or what will be the least offensive or feather-ruffling to your people? Maybe it's by what will bring in the most money or what looks best on social media? We must be reminded of Paul's words when he said pleasing people isn't the goal. Pleasing God is the goal.

William Temple was an English Anglican priest who wasn't afraid to stand up for the poor and downtrodden. Known for his concern for social justice, he became a voice of influence known all over the world. He is famously quoted for saying, "The Church is the only society on earth that exists for the benefit of non-members."[6] Think about that for a minute. When the church seeks what the people want, do those outside of the church benefit in any way? There may be some preferences that people benefit from: comfy chairs, upbeat songs, etc. However, do these preferences benefit the spiritual condition of those outside our churches? Getting closer to home, I'd ask you: when your church seeks what the people want, do people in your community benefit? It feels like a harsh question, but we all have to ask it. If they don't, you're not alone. I stand before you today saying this was us–this was our church. It's hard admitting such difficult

---

6 Temple, William. "Letter from the Archbishop of the West Indies." Theology, vol. 59, 1956.

truths, but once we come to grips with it, we can choose to get on our knees and discover what the Lord wants for both our churches and our communities.

Lastly, a multiplying church culture *operates as a community*. Before coming to our current church, our family lived in the fastest-growing community in the nation. The Bakken oil boom caused our city to double in population size in a very short amount of time. It wasn't a large city to start, and its structure was not prepared for such rapid growth. It brought our own little Wild West many complications. I remember standing in a Walmart check-out line for over an hour to buy my groceries while my two-year-old daughter ate many of the snacks in the cart I planned on buying. Lack of staffing brought shelves that once held loaves of bread and cereal boxes sitting completely empty while pallets of food were parked in the aisles still sealed shut. With many warnings that our city's water plant was at capacity and the housing market was through the roof, oddly enough, the negatives didn't compare to the positives of our quaint town. We were a transplanted family warmly welcomed by the locals. They had been through two previous booms and understood the nature of the business. Instead of being exclusive and not allowing transplants into their lives, they opened their doors as they received us into their families. A community, no matter its rate of growth, needs to be inclusive in order to grow. The church is no different. A healthy community grows by including others.

Culture sets the tone for everything a church does and is known for. Like my sister's flower farm, when our church culture is healthy, its growth provides both function and beauty. We want to actively reach our communities, helping people grow in their walk with the Lord, and coming alongside families as they learn what it looks like to follow Jesus together. These families are not just moms and dads claiming Christianity; they're kids who are learning from their parents what it looks like to come to Jesus in both the good and bad seasons of our lives and glorify Him with the outcome. Instead of being bogged down by squabbles centered on preferences, methodology, and selfish ambitions, we can flourish as we follow the vision for the church given by God Himself. When the body of believers lives in a healthy environment, there are so many reasons to celebrate. We will see people being the temperature they were made to be–accomplishing the things God has called them to do. If your church isn't there yet, it's okay. There's hope!

Laodicea got the smackdown from Jesus; there is no denying that. As I walked the grounds of this ancient city, I was given the opportunity to see the inside of a home belonging to a very wealthy family during the third century. In a time when Christianity was illegal, this particular family converted a room in their home and turned it into a church. They had secretive ways of knowing who was safe to enter their home, were well aware of the risk they were taking, and allowed their home to be a place others could gather and worship. You could see the heart of this family in the care they had for this room, and for their fellow believers. It was one of many others–proof the church of Laodicea seemingly turned from their identity we read in the letter found in Revelation. By 363 CE, the church grew to be known for its desire for strong doctrine and righteous living. They heeded Jesus' words and once again became a church that was the right temperature for the sake of the Gospel. Our churches can also be proof of the story not yet finished. We, too, can become strong pillars with firm foundations as we spread the Good News throughout the earth. Whether it's a neighbor across the street or the barista we see each morning; people will come to know Jesus because believers shared with them about their own spiritual transformation–not hoarding the Gospel for themselves. You and I can do the same.

God, stir a fervor in us. Stir in our churches the heart of compassion, that will share both love and truth, as we disciple others.

Reflection Questions:

- How are you allowing people in your church to discover God's truths?
- How do you make sure decisions made for your church or ministry are where God is leading you?
- Is your church or ministry growing? Why or why not?

CHAPTER THREE

OUT FROM BEHIND THE COUNTER

"The harvest is great, but the workers are few. So pray to the Lord who is in charge of the harvest; ask him to send more workers into his fields." —*Luke 10:2*

My boys love baseball. Our summer days consist of either watching, playing, or practicing for games. The car is littered with extra gear, from balls to cleats, and most notably smelly socks. Their love goes beyond those summer days at the field, though. Between my sons and my husband, our house seems to live and breathe this American pastime year-round. If we aren't watching a game, we're discussing it. From the beginning of spring training to the final game of the World Series, they are all in. In the off-season, you can find them playing a virtual rendition of the game, whether it's *Baseball 9* on the iPad or *MLB The Show* on the XBox, they are building a team of winners to shine under the lights of their favorite game.

It started when they were very young. My husband would show them his treasured Kirby Puckett trading cards from his childhood after telling them the story of watching the Minnesota Twins win it all in the 1991 World Series. As a nine-year-old boy himself, he remembers sitting on his living room floor for every game in the series. Watching his favorite player on the big box screen only fueled his love for the game. His lifelong devotion to the Twins anchored itself deep within him when he watched Puckett hit a game-winning home run on a 2-1 count off Charlie Leibrandt, giving them hope for a World Series ring as Jack Buck announced, "And we'll see you tomorrow night!" for Game 7. Nothing makes a little boy love a game more than watching his childhood hero win it all. This loyalty transferred to our boys and now runs deep within their bones. To be a Dangerfield is to be a Twins fan. And based on their bedroom decor, clothing choices, and fantasy teams, they are Dangerfields through and through.

Watching the game is enjoyable. With the sun licking your skin, mustard dripping off a freshly grilled hot dog, and children learning how to crack sunflower seeds, it's easy to find yourself falling in love with this diamond sport. However, if you talk with my boys, you will discover there's something even greater than watching a baseball game. It's playing the game. For them, feeling the dirt on their hands and getting grass stains on their pristine white pants is a much better option. Still young, they are learning a lot about what it looks like to play on a team, to anticipate plays, and to give their all. They know they're not professionals, yet they will still talk pitch grips, bat weights, and glove stitching for hours.

Why? Because being in the game is a preferred alternative to sitting in the spectators' seats at a game.

I imagine the disciples felt the same way when Jesus sent them two-by-two to proclaim the Good News of the Gospel. They were still fairly new followers of Jesus, yet equipped with everything they needed as they traveled the countryside, healing others and calling for repentance. They watched Jesus in those early years as He healed, restored, and extended forgiveness to the multitudes. They heard Him proclaim, "...My child, your sins are forgiven. ...So I will prove to you that the Son of Man has the authority on earth to forgive sins. ...Stand up, pick up your mat, and go home!" (Mark 2:5-11). It must have been thrilling to watch and witness all the prophecies they heard as children come to fruition. However, what would have been more fun than watching Him minister to others? Getting to participate in the life-changing restoration of so many themselves. Traveling from community to community, they entered the homes and streets of those who had not heard about the Messiah being amongst them—in the flesh.

The disciples had skin in the game. Like my boys' outer bruises and scrapes from the ball field, they had inner bruises and scrapes as people denied their message or pushed them away. They hurt, but they kept themselves in the game because they knew it was worth it. Jesus even told them to shake the dust from their feet and move on to the next community if it was necessary. **We don't stop because we've been wounded.** We keep going—because the message is too great to use excuses to stop. As the disciples kept moving forward, despite their hurts, leaving the four walls of their own comfort, they came home with incredible reports of being able to preach the good news, bring healing to the sick, and even cast out demons. Thankfully, they didn't allow excuses to convince them to give up and head back home. Praise God!

Are you, as a leader, participating in the ministry? No... not the ministry you're paid to do. The ministry of life transformation every believer is called to do. I know you're busy. It's difficult. Your focus is your staff and board. Your role is to "equip the saints to do the work of the ministry." The last time you tried, it backfired. Let's just call all of these what they are—excuses. No title or position supersedes our first mandate as believers to reach the lost. We can sit back and encourage those we lead to do this, like the manager watching from the dugout, hoping they do what we want, or we can jump onto the field ourselves, get stains on our pants, dirt on our hands, and join in.

Over the last year, Dan and I mastered using the McDonalds app. It's a skill, I know. Whether this is something to be proud of or ashamed of, we have saved hundreds of dollars using the app when we are traveling or need a quick way to feed little growling stomachs. We've even made a game out of how little we can spend when we visit the famous golden arches. This game has alternatively helped feed my desires for other things like coffee or colorful Paper Mate Inkjoy pens. Regrettably, Dan often reminds me we actually aren't saving any money at all because of these so-called "needs."

Often, we will walk into a McDonalds to pick up an order we made, only to find people standing at the kiosks confused on how to order. Whether they want to use their rewards points or still pay for their order in cash, they stand in the lobby confused by machines at the front door. Taking away customer service employees from the front desk has not helped the issue. Unfortunately, most of today's McDonald's employees are busy doing their assembly line work and not noticing the flustered customers in their store. The lack of personnel in the lobby leaves a lot of ignored and frustrated customers.

I understand why the decision was made to make all orders digital, as it saves the company money and doesn't require as many employees on the premises at one time. From a financial standpoint, it's completely understandable. The problem is, while most Americans like quick and easy, we also like to receive help when we need it and are rather impatient when it's not available.

The other day, we headed in (like I said, we go often enough it could be considered embarrassing) to pick up an order we made to grab and go. Walking in, we saw our order wasn't quite ready, so we found a seat to wait while they finished preparing it. While waiting for our order, we discovered a couple standing at the kiosk looking quite lost. With no employees available to help them, they kept pressing the touching screen over and over with no progress. Dan eventually walked up to them and asked if they needed any help. Their first response was, "Do you work here?" He laughed and said that while he wasn't an employee, he had become quite efficient with McDonalds ordering. He showed them how to use the deals from their app, as well as redeem rewards, and how the different forms of payment work with the kiosk. Grateful for his assistance, they ordered their fries and ice cream as we went on our way.

We aren't employees at our favorite fast food stop. We weren't required to come from behind a counter and help a customer. But seeing confused and frustrated faces, we stopped to help. Not expecting a thank you from the staff or even a free Diet Coke (I mean, I would've taken it if they had offered), we chose to help because assistance was required for this couple to get their coveted milkshake.

Our cities are filled with people who are looking for help, who are wanting to know their purpose for being on this earth. Unlike our time at McDonalds, as followers of Jesus, we are expected to step from behind the counter and help those who are lost and need direction. Our counter is the four walls of our church. When we stay within these walls, we are missing a whole world of opportunity. Literally.

Creating a culture of disciples who make disciples requires us, as leaders, to lead the way. Choosing to have skin in the game, walking out of our buildings, and intentionally looking for the lost and confused allows us to come alongside those we may never otherwise meet–to give them hope and direction. They may not walk away with a milkshake, but they will walk away knowing there's a God who loves them and pursues them to the ends of the earth.

Ananias was one who chose to lead the way. Saul had just had his blinding experience with Jesus on the road to Damascus and was brought to the city with no plan on how to move forward from it. The Lord approached Ananias in a vision and said, "...Go over to Straight Street, to the house of Judas. When you get there, ask for a man from Tarsus named Saul. He is praying to me right now. I have shown him a vision of a man named Ananias coming in and laying hands on him so he can see again" (Acts 9:11-12). Ananias was terrified. He knew this Saul of Tarsus and what he was capable of. He had heard the horrific stories of what happened to believers in the holy city as a result of Saul's word. Nonetheless, the Lord was clear–Ananias needed to go to Saul. God had big, well-thought-out plans on how to use Saul to bring the message of hope to all the people of the world.

Imagine being in the shoes of Ananias at this time. God was asking him to go to the one man who was relentlessly trying to destroy the message of Jesus. He was nothing like the disciples of Jesus Ananias knew–he was filled with righteous anger and religious pride. Yet God said, "Go!" It had to have been incredibly uncomfortable.

Yet he chose to walk in obedience despite his fears (and probably against the advice of others in his life).

Scripture says, "So Ananias went and found Saul. He laid his hands on him and said, "Brother Saul, the Lord Jesus, who appeared to you on the road, has sent me so that you might regain your sight and be filled with the Holy Spirit." Instantly something like scales fell from Saul's eyes, and he regained his sight" (Acts 9:17-18). Someone had to receive Saul. Someone had to walk out from behind the counter, leave the four walls of their religious safety net, and receive a man who desperately needed healing. Someone had to sit with him and teach him in the ways of Jesus–not just religiosity. Understanding his role as a disciple, to both walk in obedience and bring people to the feet of Jesus, Ananias did just that.

I love how Scripture says, "...something like scales fell from Saul's eyes." In my mind, I envision his eyes going from a cloudy gray back to bright brown eyes. While witnessing the physical change, I imagine there was an added spark in his expression. Not only could he physically see, but he was also given the opportunity to spiritually see the power of Jesus. If this man called Christ could heal someone physically, without even being present, He could heal someone inwardly as well. What if Ananias hadn't gone searching for Saul? Would God have asked someone else to go? Or would the disciples have begun the slippery slope toward casual Christianity? Is it possible you and I wouldn't be serving in the capacity we are today because most of us are Gentiles who would have never heard about the restoring power of Jesus? It's a lot of "ifs," but we have to consider the impact of stepping out of our four walls–to go in search of the Sauls who still don't know about God's ability to heal the deepest places inside us.

There are modern-day Sauls all around us. They may not be as bold or aggressive as the Saul we see in Acts, arresting and imprisoning followers of Jesus, but they are just as lost and in need of an Ananias. One option is to sit in our worship centers with our finely tuned sound systems, secure children's ministries, and perfectly brewed coffee and hope they come to us. We do this. You do this. But we both know how it's working. The other option is to model our life after Ananias, who "went and found" someone living in darkness. And as we do this, just maybe, those who we lead will follow. Like Megan, for example.

Years ago, I met Megan. We first met when her family started coming to our church. Wishing there was more to a relationship with God than what they were experiencing and learning at a previous church they attended, they chose to check out a few others in town to see if what they were hungry and searching for was even something they could discover. After their first visit to our church, they found themselves walking through our doors week after week. Between the messages, the worship, and the community they found, her family soon realized what they were searching for was indeed available to them–and they wanted more.

Hesitant to dive in too quickly, they quietly sat in our services for over a year before trying out a small group. Coincidentally, the small group Megan landed in was mine. Every week, we met in my home as we learned about hard-to-reach places, unreached people groups, and the specific needs of missionaries our church supported. We would pray for these global workers and then go into a time of teaching on having a missional mindset in our very own city. It was in this small group I learned of her heart for missions. Her family had been on a number of mission trips over the years, and they deeply desired to take what they learned on those trips and apply it in our own community. However, there was one problem. Megan was terrified of praying out loud with people. She knew in order to do ministry work, it would require her to pray with others, and it kept her from moving forward. She could pray with her husband or with her children in the comfort of the four walls of her home, and even in the church if she was persuaded enough. I mean, these are places you're supposed to pray, right? But outside of them? That was a different story.

Each week, as we heard from missionaries about their immediate needs, we would pray. It was often just two of us in our group who were willing to pray out loud, while the rest just chose to agree with us. Knowing God had more for Megan and the others in our group, I determined it was time to stretch myself. If anything, to lead by example, so they would see how they could grow into the potential God had for them. Praying out loud for others wasn't necessarily scary to me, so what was? And was I willing to do it for the sake of the Gospel?

Finding a new story to share each week, I told my group how I prayed with a stranger at the store checkout line or how I overheard a conversation and stepped in to share how God helped me through a similar situation. As an introvert, I found talking to strangers wasn't easy for me—my group could testify to that. Trying to help boost their boldness, we would pray that God would give us all the gentle push we needed to take hold of every opportunity—praying God would literally bring someone our way to share Jesus with each week. Even if it meant a stranger.

I'll never forget the week Megan walked in my front door with her husband. She had the largest grin plastered on her face. My curiosity was piqued. "Megan, what are you so happy about?" I asked. Immediately, she stepped into my living room, still dressed in her winter coat and boots, and responded exuberantly, "I can't wait till the end of the group to tell you: I prayed with someone! OUT LOUD!" We laughed. We celebrated. We clapped and jumped for joy! She stepped out of her safe prayer spaces and stepped into a whole new world of Jesus-following. It was amazing! Without realizing it, Megan started a ripple effect in our group. We no longer just prayed for opportunities; we started looking for opportunities. Week after week, we would share how God brought someone new into our life we were able to share the Gospel with, or brought opportunities with co-workers as doors once impossible to open were now being unlatched.

It didn't stop there for Megan. As her boldness to pray grew, so did her heart of compassion. Listening to the stories of hurting and struggling people did more than compel her to pray; they compelled her to action. Recognizing their physical needs, she began to look for ways to help fill those insufficiencies. Whether it was a couch, a set of pots and pans, or clothing for their children, she knew God had called her to do more than pray.

Almost daily now, Megan prays with people. She serves those struggling in our community and who are looking for a fresh start. She looks them in the eye as she listens to their stories. She hugs them, thanks them for sharing, steps into their struggle, and says, "Let me tell you where I found hope." The likelihood of Megan meeting these people in a church is low. Whether from past hurts, fear of the unknown, or simply not interested, they probably would've never walked through a church's doors before meeting her. Megan would've never had the opportunity to shed Christ's light on their situations. However, because she understands her role as a believer is to share the Gospel everywhere she goes, she takes the message outside of the church and brings it with her into the community.

Megan's life is a perfect example of the impact a leader can have on the culture of their church and how others begin to live out their faith as a disciple. The men and women who met in my home weekly needed to be stretched, but instead of choosing to preach it, I chose to live it. Discipleship programs in our churches are wonderful. Small groups that do topical studies, Bible studies, or even are activity-based allow people to build relationships with like-minded people. Church attendees are able to grow in their understanding of Scripture, and it allows them the chance to be better equipped to share what they learn. But if our churches lack a culture of multiplication, these groups rarely grow, and they rarely equip others with the understanding of how to disciple someone else. Without intentionality, they become a place to consume instead of a place to help work out their salvation like Paul mentions in the letter of Philippians. They often ask their church family to "Come and see" without charging them to "Go and do."

I believe one reason why we don't see ministry leaders intentionally sharing the Good News outside of their four walls is because they're busy. Between preparing messages, leading small groups, pouring into team members, meeting the immediate and emergent needs of their congregation, plus giving attention to their spouses and/or families... yikes! Who has time to be intentional with anything else? I've felt a similar weight. I wake up at the crack of dawn just to spend time with Jesus—when would I find time to share Him with others outside of all my other responsibilities as a pastor and a parent? Once I settled into this ministerial role better, however, I discovered the weight I felt was a pressure I had actually

LEADING SPIRITUAL HOARDERS

put on myself. As a ministry leader, I've learned to think in terms of structure. Classes. Attendance. Curriculum. Preaching. Teaching. Assimilation. The thought of finding someone outside of my church to disciple rushes in the belief that I have to formulate a step-by-step plan to show this person who Christ is. It became "Just another thing to do." But what if that wasn't the case?

Knowing I couldn't add more to my calendar, I wanted to find a way to share Jesus in the midst of what I was already doing. Whether it was a brief conversation or a consistent time of discipleship, I knew it was something that needed to be a priority in my life–for both my walk with God and for the sake of our church's culture. I had to ask myself, 'What was I already doing?' I was taking my daughter to swim practice and my boys to baseball practice. I was taking the kids to the library weekly. I went to the grocery store every Thursday evening. I walked past neighbors on my way to the mailbox every day after school pick-up. I went to the same exact gas station every few days for gas or a Diet Coke. I met up with educators at PTO meetings. Need I keep going? Maybe I couldn't be intentional to disciple every single person I saw on a weekly basis, but what if I chose one person? Not wanting to treat them like a target, I began to partner with the Holy Spirit as I prayed for opportunities to build relationships with others. I would share stories of my kids and how much we loved our new city while also hearing their stories about family, careers, and interests, listening for any clues that led me to believe they were searching. All of a sudden, what once felt like a burden became something I looked forward to. God's mission welling up inside me, I would wake up each morning and ask God, "Who do we get to talk to today?" I had skin in the game. I was ready to take the message outside my workplace and into my living space. And that's when I noticed Autumn.

I had become quite the regular at my local chiropractic office. At least twice a month, I would stroll in, chat it up with the receptionist, and get myself aligned. Whether it was raining, the sun shining, or I was trudging through a foot of snow, I would faithfully show up to each appointment. My chiropractor would listen to my antics as I would come up with some wild story about why I had to waltz through his clinic again. We would talk about family, school, and even church. While I'm still working on him to come visit us on a Sunday, he has been nothing but supportive of all the things we have done for our community. Like myself, he has a heart for the people he calls his neighbors.

After he would finish with my appointment, he would send me to Autumn, who gave me all the exercises I was supposed to do in order to help with my healing. Please note I said, "supposed to." Every time I came in, I was confident Autumn knew I never did a lick of my stretches. Despite this knowledge, she'd still patiently go through each movement with me to guarantee I knew how to do them on the chance I decided to do them.

I saw Autumn frequently. She seemed like a fun-loving girl, but I really knew nothing about her. One particular Sunday, I walked out of our worship center a little early to greet people as they left, and as I stepped out, my eyes widened at the sight of Autumn. What was she doing at church? Had I invited her? No... I think it was just my chiropractor I invited. I later discovered some of her friends had invited her, and despite my initial noticing of her, it wasn't her first time there. Oddly enough, they invited her, and even though they no longer attend, she kept finding herself back in our worship center every few weeks. Knowing I needed to be more intentional with my everyday moments, I began to pray about how I could develop a relationship with Autumn outside of my pure aversion to stretching.

I didn't know Autumn's story. I didn't know where she stood when it came to religion or Jesus. I didn't even know if she liked me or was annoyed by me. However, I knew God was asking me to step into her world. So one day, I asked her to lunch. One lunch turned into many. We shared each other's stories. We laughed. We cried. We prayed. And we read Scripture together. I watched as Autumn's demeanor began to change with each meal, literally witnessing her life transform before my eyes. She longed to know Jesus and for Jesus to know her. She was hungry–hungry to have a life that actually had meaning. Praise God, over time, she found that meaning in Him.

Recently she wrote me a little note. She said, "I never had someone older than me reach out and truly be there for me. I was so stuck with life until you reached out. Thank you for lighting my fire for Jesus and letting me experience true support." Friends, it wasn't me–you and I both know it. It was God pursuing her through me. It was His support she felt; I was just lucky enough to observe it.

Many of us may deny it, but our buildings become an excuse. If we're not careful, we will miss the greatest opportunities God lays in our laps. I saw Autumn at least twice a month for over a year. It wasn't until I saw her walk within the four walls of our church did I even think to approach her about faith conversations. I almost missed it! I grieve at the thought of it. I'm as guilty as any when I put too much confidence in our strong church programming. We can begin to feel like we're doing pretty good for ourselves. Our students are sitting under the teaching of Sunday School teachers and small group leaders. Our adults are going through Growth Tracks and Bible studies. Sadly, the message begins to lose its effectiveness when it isn't carried outside the doors after said programming. Like it was for me, many rarely step outside the building and actively search for the one God wants to encounter.

I also think we find ourselves in this man-made predicament because once a church is seasoned and has been established for quite some time, it begins to lose its fervor if its leaders don't stay vigilant in its purpose. The church we lead is over 100 years old. Without sounding crass, it's easy to become comfortable with how we do church. Church plants, on the other hand, have a running DNA of taking the message outside the four walls of the church—otherwise, they'd have very empty rooms. A church planter knows that in order to grow the church they are required to go into their communities. They need to listen to the stories of their people and share the love of Christ in any way possible. However, what happens when, years down the road, this church plant is now in a permanent space? What happens when they are a healthy size, with a healthy budget, and by all appearances have healthy programming? The pastor can pivot from sharing to maintaining.

Whether we've inherited a church or started it from the ground up, remaining attentive to the call and purpose of the church will keep us in the mindset that ministry doesn't just happen inside the four walls of the church. Sitting back and being a spectator, like at a local baseball game, keeps us locked into the mindset of how ministry can only happen inside the church building. This mindset gives us permission to hoard the Gospel. Instead, we need to be like the disciples and get into the game. It doesn't have to be an organized ministry. It could be simply choosing to stop by your neighbor's house on your way to the mailbox every day for a 5-10 minute chat. Over time, as we partner with the Holy Spirit, we have no idea what kind of doors He will open up for Gospel conversations because we chose to remain watchful and open. The Autumns of this world are just waiting for someone to tell them there's hope.

Reflection Questions:

- Is stepping out from 'behind the counter' something that comes naturally to you? Why or why not?

- Do you have room in your schedule to intentionally pour into someone who's in your community? Why or why not?

- What is a recent story or testimony of someone getting saved outside of your church?

CHAPTER FOUR

THE LEADER'S HEART

"You have heard me teach things that have been confirmed by many reliable witnesses. Now teach these truths to other trustworthy people who will be able to pass them on to others." —*2 Timothy 2:2*

We were slowing down to a stoplight when a car pulled up next to us. Littered with obscene stickers on the windows and rear bumper, my kids stared at the car as if trying to figure out some cryptic code. Mortified by the images I saw, I encouraged the kids to look in the other direction at anything I could quickly find to redirect their attention. But it was too late. The driver had seen disgust written all over my face. We soon discovered he was not only upset with my reaction, he also felt the need to make a statement against my marked disapproval. Once the light turned green, he stepped hard on the gas, moving forward so he would be directly in front of us by the next red light. As we nervously sat waiting for the light to turn green, the driver ahead of us put his car in reverse, swiftly backed into our car, and bolted forward as soon as the light changed. We were stunned. Did that man just purposely back into our vehicle?

At the next intersection, I quickly jumped out of our vehicle to see if there was any damage. Nearby drivers rolled down their windows and asked if we were okay. Then they asked the same question we had: "What in the world just happened?!" Thankfully, no damage was done, but it opened our eyes to see how our coming to our new city was about more than leading a church–it was about revitalizing a body God was going to use to do some damage to the kingdom of hell. And Satan knew it.

Those first couple of years we discovered some stark differences in the roles of lead pastor and staff pastor. Serving as staff pastors over the years, we helped carry out the vision God gave our lead pastor. We planned our events, our messages, and our small group gatherings based on where the church was headed. It kept us busy and gave us a road map to follow. When people within the church had an issue with something we planned or did, we were able to listen to them and respond by letting them know we chose to go the route we did because we were following the vision of our pastor. It was an easy out for us when interacting with those who cared more about preferences than they did about the health of the church as a whole. It also gave us the ability to move past the frustration and still easily love those in the church well–it wasn't personal.

We've now learned how the weight of the lead pastor role is much different. While we carried the fishing pole and tackle box as staff, so to speak, our boss was pulling the boat. The day our car was backed into by an angry driver at the stoplight was a curt way of reminding us we were now the ones who pulled the boat. Choosing to say yes to leading God's people wasn't going to give us a posh life. It was going to take sweat and tears. What we did, how we lived, and the decisions we made would have an impact on the church. When the church grew and strengthened, it would ultimately have an impression on our lives as well. We continuously see the fruit of this today: when God is moving in the hearts of people in our church, it upsets Satan. He goes after the leadership, as well as the staff, and over time it impacts the church. While this was more obscure, the incident at the stoplight made it very clear to us. We were now living proof of the weight our new role carried.

It's easy to allow hard situations to jade us and allow our hearts to grow cold. I could've gone to bed that night angry with God for sending us somewhere "filled with hateful people." I could've tried to swoop in to protect my children from the world and, ultimately, myself. Hard things can change our perspective; our guards can rise higher than an eight-foot fence, and our ability to trust others can wane. Sadly, this was the first of many unfortunate events over the first few years. The car incident was small in comparison as we proceeded to experience health diagnoses, false accusations, and betrayal from friends. These circumstances confirmed time and time again the enemy was fighting for our church and our city. With no doubt in my mind, I believe he understood if he could get the church off mission, just like the church in Laodicea, we read about in the last chapter, we wouldn't be a threat to his work. In our case, what the enemy didn't know was that this church he was fighting for had leaders who were not only stubborn, they knew God had called them to break spiritual barriers in their community. Instead of thinking about ourselves and what made us comfortable, our family chose to take on this fight with God on our side.

Stepping into this unfamiliar position, we understood in order for others to align their lives with God, and the tasks He has given them, leading them by example, was what would drive the mission home. The cultivated ground of our church's heart directly correlated with our own hearts as its leaders. We knew this. It was preached to us all the time by other leaders and conference speakers.

A few years ago, I had the opportunity to meet and sit under the teaching of John Maxwell. My husband Dan and I were attending a pastoral retreat centered mostly around doubling the church's impact for God's kingdom. I was thrilled to glean from him and found myself moved when I heard him say, "A leader is one who knows the way, goes the way, and shows the way." When we go the way and show the way, it reminds us how pastors should not be leading out of a title–**we should be leading out of a heart burning for those who are without a relationship with Jesus.** There's a different weight we carry with that title, but it doesn't change our status as a follower of Jesus.

Equipping those in our church to share the Gospel is ultimately the goal. However, in order to create a culture of disciples who make disciples in our churches, we have to be disciples who make disciples. We have to walk away from our jaded mindsets, be willing to revitalize our own perspectives, and pull up our bootstraps as we step into a world desperately in need of a Savior. Creating a multiplying culture begins with the leaders of the church—it starts with the top. Are you, as a ministry leader, spending one-on-one time with those who are curious about faith? Maybe they haven't taken any steps forward yet in their walk with God, and they simply need someone to come alongside them and show them the way. Unfortunately, many pastors state they don't have the time. Whether they are the sole pastor on staff or one of many, they often mention this is why they have discipleship programs in their church structure. The pastor can't do it all, right? So, we teach in groups to help us get more bang for our buck. Frequently hearing this, Dan and I questioned how we could bring those in our church to an understanding of their role as a follower of Jesus. How could we convince them their job was also to disciple others toward Him, especially if we weren't doing it ourselves?

Nehemiah was the cupbearer to King Artaxerxes in the 5th Century BCE. The Babylonian exile was over, and when he asked about the Jewish remnant, he was given terrible news. He had been told there was great trouble for those who returned to Judah; the wall of Jerusalem had been torn down, and the gates set ablaze. His heart was broken, mourning as he wept over the destruction. Choosing to fast and pray, he asked the Lord to remember his people whom he redeemed and to give Nehemiah what he needed in order to make a positive difference in the lives of those left defenseless. He may not have been a Jewish ruler, but as a high-ranking official in the Persian Empire, he knew his position could help bring restoration–if God was willing to have him do so.

Four months after hearing the tragic news, the awaited opportunity presented itself. The king recognized Nehemiah's grief, asked him what was wrong, and took the time to listen to the request of his official. Nehemiah asked him, "If it pleases the king, and if you are pleased with me, your servant, send me to Judah to rebuild the city where my ancestors are buried" (Nehemiah 2:5). After the king granted permission, Nehemiah left with the animal he rode, letters from the king, and a few men by his side.

Inspecting the walls, Nehemiah began to devise a restoration plan. God brought him men from all over the region–nearby priests, nobles, and other officials–to lead as they rebuilt the city walls. The Jews were thrilled to see their walls finding repair because they knew this wall meant safety for their people. Yet, the other officials were upset. Men like Sanballat, Tobiah, and Gresham were often noted for mocking Nehemiah and his men, disturbed someone would care about the welfare of the Jews. This did not deter Nehemiah, however. He knew

God had called him to lead this group of men to rebuild the wall, and because he cared for the people, he was determined not to let anything stop him. He held his head high with the men, as each section was mended and reconstructed. When they met opposition, Nehemiah prayed fervently. When they were scorned, he stood by his men's side, building the wall by day and guarding it by night. He wasn't a leader who sat on a pedestal somewhere and gave orders on how to rebuild. He stood with them, sweating and laboring alongside them, until fifty-two days later when the walls were completed.

Nehemiah understood his role, and he was willing to fight to the death to complete his task. We have a task, too; as pastors, we are to lead the body of Christ. We will face opposition from both in and outside of the church. If we don't know what our role entails, we will succumb to the pressure and find ourselves comfortable with simply standing behind a pulpit.

I'll be the first to admit that being a leader can be intimidating. We have nothing to hide behind when things get tough. It can be easy to become passive or even a people-pleaser because the fear of opposition is too much. We entered ministry because we love people, but we never anticipated the people not loving us back. Friends, we can't hide behind a pulpit. Our platform may allow us to preach the Gospel to those within the walls of our church, but if we don't share it outside its walls, we are simply hoarding it to ourselves. We must step away from the podium, stage, lectern, or whatever you preach from on a Sunday morning and step into the streets of our cities. We may not be rebuilding walls and physically guarding the safety of our people, but what we are doing is carrying the Gospel to a dark and weary world. The weight we feel isn't a burden we are meant to carry alone. Like Nehemiah, we bring the burden of leadership to the feet of Christ. He will lead our hearts and our hands, and help us remain focused on the task at hand, so we can continue the work of making Jesus known.

During our years in the KidMin world, Dan and I were given the opportunity to work with a couple named Eric and Liz Hoffman. Eric is the NextGen Missions Director with the Assemblies of God, while Liz works for an incredible organization called World Serve International, helping solve the world water crisis. When we first met them years ago, we instantly felt a bond with this couple as we spoke at a summer kids camp in Illinois. Well before we were introduced to them, they left their position in the local church to take a state-wide ministry position. At the time we met, their role was to help students all across their state raise funds for worldwide missions. They worked hard, streamlining both the children and youth missions departments, knowing if all the students worked together, they could accomplish so much more than they already were. No longer did they want students competing with one another in their giving. Instead, they wanted them to join their efforts for an even greater impact. With each step they took, and decision they made, they saw student involvement and giving increase. But they weren't satisfied. As they traveled throughout Illinois, they saw an incredible amount of untapped potential in students. Trying to figure out how to draw it out of them, they began looking at the leaders. Eric and Liz knew if they led these children and youth leaders by example, then they, in turn, would lead their own students by the same example.

Wanting to see God move without them getting in the way, they chose to fast and pray. Eric and Liz believed a person doesn't prevail by their own strength, but rather, God would lead the way if they remained faithful (1 Samuel 2:9-10). Instead of fasting food, their family chose to fast their finances. Each month, they would pay for their essentials: food, shelter, water, etc., but things like clothing, entertainment, and dining at restaurants were out of the question. For an entire year, their family fasted what was unnecessary so they could give as much as possible to missions. It was an incredible act of faith, knowing God would multiply their money given and still provide for their daily needs. They didn't publicly boast about their financial fast, nor did they deny people when they asked why they weren't buying items like birthday and Christmas gifts. They knew God was calling them to do something more drastic, and they gladly led the way as they rose to the challenge God put before them.

Every Easter, the Hoffmans had a tradition of filling a basket for their kids to find on Resurrection Sunday. Their children knew a basket wouldn't be coming that particular year because, instead, they were choosing to help provide materials and modes of transportation for missionaries to share the Gospel wherever they served. While they were sad, the kids understood the mission. However, lo and behold, the Lord honored their sacrifice, and on Easter morning, the children found Easter baskets brimming with gifts and goodies on their doorstep. Someone saw the sacrifice they were making and wanted to bless them for their efforts. The Hoffmans didn't choose to fast for the earthly rewards but rather for the spiritual prize coming from it by way of the leaders serving under them. Incredibly, God chose to bless them with a little earthly gift too. The following year, they discovered their leaders' givings increased exponentially, with students coming on board with even more the following year. This money helped many missionaries bring the Good News to hard-reached places all over the globe, but the purpose of their efforts was for much more. The goal was really the heart of the leaders and students. Eric and Liz knew if they could reach the heart, God would have their attention as they walked in step with Him daily. Because of their willingness to respond to God's challenge, many leaders and students are still living a life filled with spiritual fruit today, as they now lead others in cultivating a heart for missions.

Through stories like Nehemiah and the Hoffmans, we are reminded yet again of the importance of leaders who lead by example. If we anticipate a culture of disciples who make disciples within our churches, we cannot expect it to happen organically if all we personally do is use the pulpit to get the point across. As a leader, we are called to equip the saints. Before that, however, we are followers of Jesus who are called to make disciples. So, let's take our leader's hat off and look at ourselves as followers of Jesus. Are you taking the time to share the Gospel in your everyday life? Does your community know you merely as a pastor, or do they know you by the faith you live out daily? Do they know you love your community and have a heart for seeing it thrive?

When we choose to be intentional as we meet pre-believers, doors of opportunity will fly open to share Christ in new and fresh ways. I can tell you from personal experience that there is nothing like sitting at a table with an acquaintance from your community as the realization kicks in how deeply Jesus loves them. Sitting over a coffee or a sandwich, I have shed tears with friends, parents of my children's friends, and even medical personnel as they share their heartbreaking stories. Filled with past hurts and current pains, I have been trusted to share hope with them and have been given the freedom to show them the way of Jesus. We cannot deny the power of one-on-one discipleship.

In 1903, there was a young 21-year-old Italian man named Charles Ponzi. Charles immigrated to the United States with only $2.50 in his pocket and dreamed of striking it rich in this new opportunistic country. Once he arrived, Charles worked a variety of jobs to earn some hard, cold cash, but it wasn't helping him meet the dreams he wanted to pursue. It wasn't until 1919 that this charming young man started to see a breakthrough for his hopes, and even some international fame. Opening a business in Boston, he promoted the sales of international reply coupons. These coupons made it possible for people to buy all sorts of international postage stamps for a discounted price. He had this great plan of buying the stamps in bulk from Europe, and then inflating those prices for the Americans who would gladly purchase them. Promising a 50% return for those who would like to buy in, he began making promises–promises he couldn't keep. Business was booming but without a well thought-out plan, it landed him in prison. Maybe you've figured it out by now, but the phrase we use today–Ponzi scheme–originates from this unorganized entrepreneur.[7]

It's unfortunate how people like Charles cause others to be leery of someone else's validity. For example, my inbox often tells me I am the lucky winner of a new generator, am eligible for a short-term loan from the bank, and my name came up for a premium knife set reward all in one day. Lucky me, right? If only that were true. It's fatiguing, being bombarded day after day by lies from imposters who are trying to lure me for their own benefit. These lies and schemes in every little avenue cause me to be anxious as I try to distinguish what is real or not. Whether it's through spam mail, social media, phone calls, or even personal relationships–I am fighting for discernment between an authentic and fraudulent life.

---

7 https://en.wikipedia.org/wiki/Charles_Ponzi *Please note Charles Ponzi was a lifetime criminal and this is not a literal retelling of his history.

We see fruit from a fraudulent life in people all throughout Scripture: Jacob scamming Esau for his birthright (Genesis 25), Ananias and Sapphira lying to the Holy Spirit (Acts 5), and Delilah tricking Samson out of his strength (Judges 16). While these are just a few examples, we can find many more because the Bible is filled with stories of broken people. Lies, trickery, and dishonesty come in different forms, but what remains constant despite it all is God Himself. He never changed or wavered despite their circumstances. A series of small choices eventually positioned these people to be swindled by their own motives, but God gives us the ability to live a life of authentic faith filled with dreams rooted in Him.

Daily, we run across people who are bombarded by lies and deceit, just like we are. We meet them not only in our churches but at the mailbox, the check-out line, and our kids' sporting events. Maybe they are just as exhausted and just as desperate to find a life of meaning. I think about the people I see on a daily basis outside of ministry: the old man at the grocery store, the FedEx guy, and the young mom pushing her stroller down my street. I wonder if they see Jesus in me, but maybe they're hesitant to even look because the fight for authenticity in faith feels fruitless. Is it possible they've been hurt in the past by someone in the church, or they met a sidewalk preacher who was more creepy than evangelistic? Maybe they had a grandparent who set the bar so high that instead of trying to meet it they gave up and walked away from both family and the church. Perhaps they met a Christian who didn't know how to extend the grace they talked about, choosing to tear others down for not following the law of Scripture. Just like sifting through my email, I wonder if it's exhausting looking for authentic faith. What would happen if we chose to live this authentic faith-filled life–not because we're a leader in the church, but because we are a son or daughter of Christ Himself? Would it only benefit us, or would it benefit those around us too?

Unfortunately, many pastors are living a fraudulent life when they reserve the Gospel message for the four walls of the church. They begin to see people in their communities as statistics to be counted instead of people with names and stories. Numbers are ultimately used to measure the success of their church. If we aren't careful, we can believe the church is dependent on its numerical value, choosing not to give those numbers a face and a name. When a face is attached, all of a sudden, we are held accountable for them. We are responsible for taking the time to hear their stories, do life with them, and allow our hearts to extend the grace and hope Jesus extends to us.

Jesus told Simon and Andrew to follow Him, and He would show them how to fish for people. In today's modern world, we can choose to gather fish by the net full, or we can reel them in one at a time. Both are effective, but I'll tell you what–there's nothing like catching a big ol' walleye off North Dakota's Lake Sakakawea, the third largest reservoir in the United States. A colossal walleye will fight your line for as long as he can, giving you the reel of your life. Once caught, the reward you have in the end makes you smile until your face hurts! We have people in our lives who have fought against God for various reasons. Whether from examples mentioned above or truly because of a lack of understanding. Despite their reasons, we are called to reach them. Like Simon and Andrew, Jesus is calling us to be fishers of men. When we choose to live a fraudulent life by not actively sharing the Good News outside of our four walls, we literally miss the reel of a lifetime. There is no greater earthly reward than watching someone come to know Christ because you chose to walk in obedience to the call as a follower of Him.

Our character–not our title–will be what earns the trust of those around us. From the church body to our son's baseball coach, we want to be men and women who conduct ourselves in a manner worthy of Christ. It benefits others when we both reflect and share His character instead of our own human nature. Nehemiah's character is what motivated Artaxerxes to grant his permission for the walls to be rebuilt. The king wasn't Jewish. He didn't care about the Jews, but he cared about Nehemiah. As his cupbearer, Nehemiah was a faithful man who served him well and proved himself trustworthy because he lived what he believed.

You are a cupbearer to the King as well. Instead of a wine glass and a Persian sitting on a throne, you are holding the greatest story ever told and are being held accountable by the King of all kings. You were created to reflect Him by intentionally sharing Him, not just teaching about Him. The influence you carry, whether it feels significant or not, has the potential to change an entire city filled with people. That potential is not a given, though. Just because we have a title in a place of worship amongst an entire community of people does not mean the potential will be realized.

Nehemiah's heart broke when he heard the news, which prompted him to pray. I can almost hear the tears falling to the ground as he pleaded with the Lord to hear his cries and help him when he approached the king. Do you carry the same response when you hear the news of someone living in darkness? Do you plead with the Father to hear your prayer and to use you in some capacity to shed light on their circumstances? It's easy to cast judgment on people, especially those who decide they're upset with you and back into your vehicle at a stoplight. Moments like these should serve as reminders. If our heart isn't breaking for the lost around us to the point it causes us to do something about it, how do we expect our church to care as well?

Paul wrote to the Philippians, "Above all, you must live as citizens of heaven, conducting yourselves in a manner worthy of the Good News about Christ. Then, whether I come and see you again or only hear about you, I will know that you are standing together with one spirit and one purpose, fighting together for the faith, which is the Good News" (Philippians 1:27). Imagine the day you get to heaven. If it looks anything like North Dakota, it will have the brightest sunrises, fields of gold, purple, and green, and the biggest sky you've ever seen. Sounds glorious, doesn't it? As you enter the gates, you look from your left to your right, seeing it filled with people you recognize-those who lived a life of authentic faith alongside you. Next to them, you see other people you don't know. While looking at the vast array, strangers approach you and share about the interactions they had with those you led in your community. The coffee dates and meals you shared with those who were hungry to learn more about Jesus bore fruit after all! They no longer felt the quest for truth to be fruitless because through others' lives, and ultimately yours, they learned the ways of Jesus when discipled by others. As you led from a heart desiring to disciple the one, your congregation followed suit. What a day of rejoicing that will be!

Reflection Questions:

- How have you allowed hard moments in ministry to negatively affect you?

- What did you think of Nehemiah's response to the turmoil of the Israelites? Would you respond similarly about your community?

- What breaks your heart when you think about your community?

CHAPTER FIVE

OPENING THE GATE

"We are witnesses of these things and so is the Holy Spirit, who is given by God to those who obey Him."
—*Acts 5:32*

My husband and I decided to go on our second cruise. We had so much fun the first time, it was mutually decided to give 'er a go again–but this time with friends. Looking forward to adventuring together both on our own and with our friends sounded glorious! With the rays kissing our sun-deprived skin, that's exactly what it was. We met new people as they shared their stories. We tasted new food, things we never had the opportunity to eat in North Dakota. And came back looking a tad darker and a little less Norwegian (well, my husband, anyway).

Every night, as we entered the dining hall, we were greeted by the sweetest waitress. She was from the Asia Pacific region, had an incredible smile, and (thankfully) laughed at all of our ridiculous jokes. We enjoyed each evening as we sat around our little dinner table. However, every time we reached our assigned seats, I felt the Holy Spirit nudging me. The problem was that I had no idea what He was nudging me to do until the final night. Our waitress looked me straight in the eye and, in broken English, said, "You are all happy. You smile a lot." It was a simple phrase, a compliment to how relaxed we must have been to give off such an impression. The Holy Spirit urgently impelled me, saying, "Tell her what gives you joy." In my head, I asked Him, "Now?" The inner battle inside me commenced as God continued to ask, and I kept responding with "Why?" or "How?". I felt my heart pounding through my chest, and I'm sure I looked stunned–maybe even afraid. I often told God I would do whatever He asked me to do, but this? No way! Not to a stranger.

The evening continued as I wrestled with my willingness to obey. My inner battle ensued while the conversation remained light and joyous at the table. She brought us some decadent desserts, ones I'd never be willing to pay for at home, and then cleared our plates after we gobbled them up. I watched her walk away and felt my heart breaking with every step she took. I had disobeyed the Holy Spirit, and I knew it. I chose to say nothing because my heart was too proud to do the one simple task He asked me to.

We walked back to our room. As soon as we crossed the threshold of our quaint room, I burst into tears. My poor husband was completely caught off guard and probably a little concerned too. As he asked me what was wrong, the words spilled from my lips. As a result of my disobedience, I was a wreck. I felt sick for not following through with what I was told to do. After my meltdown,

I wiped my tears from my face, stood up, and declared I needed to go find her! I had to tell her why I had joy—a joy deep within me despite the tears spilling down my face. I rushed back to the dining room and frantically looked high and low, but she was nowhere to be found. I lost my chance. My heart was in agony due to my poor decision. As I left the room, my head hung low. That evening, I told myself that as long as I chose to obey, I would never feel this way again.

Have I disobeyed since then? Oh yeah. But I learned something that day: My job as a follower of Jesus is to continually learn how to hear the voice of the Holy Spirit and to walk in obedience when He asks me to do something on His behalf. I learned then—and I continue to learn today.

There's something to be said about the condition of my heart during the time I was on the cruise. I fought with God. His request made me uncomfortable. It pushed me to do what I tried to avoid at all costs—talk to strangers. Well, strangers who don't walk through the doors of my church, that is. That's a given, right? Let's just call it what it was, though: pride. In my complacency, I refused to take on the task before me.

King Saul was proud too. He may not have argued with God while eating crab legs and escargot on a boat in the Caribbean, but his heart led him to look at his own comfort instead of walking in obedience. Saul was the anointed man for the hour. He was to lead the people in what it looked like "to fear the Lord and faithfully serve

Him" (1 Samuel 12:24). Unfortunately, he didn't lead them well.

Early in his reign, Saul went to battle against the Philistines. Previously, he had destroyed the Philistine garrison at Geba, and they were now after Israel's blood for revenge. He was commanded by the Lord to wait for Samuel before presenting an offering on Israel's behalf, but feeling the pressure, Saul decided to depend on his own understanding and ran with the sacrifice on his own. Whether he realized it or not, his pride snuck in and said, "I've got this." As he finished the burnt offering, Samuel entered the camp appalled at Saul's choice to present it before he arrived. "'How foolish!' Samuel exclaimed. 'You have not kept the command the Lord your God gave you. Had you kept it, the Lord would have established your kingdom over Israel forever. But now your kingdom must end, for the Lord has sought out a man after His own heart" (1 Samuel 13:13-14). He failed to listen and obey the voice of the Lord. This became the beginning of his prideful spiral and his life of disobedience to God's commands, which is how we remember him. Unfortunately for Saul, he spent much of his reign being tormented by an evil spirit instead of being led by God's Spirit. But it didn't have to be this way. It wasn't always this way.

Before Saul made this grievous mistake, he had an experience with the Holy Spirit. In the Old Testament, we often see the Holy Spirit would come upon a leader for a certain time, and a precise task, subsequently making miraculous things happen. For Saul, it happened shortly after meeting the prophet Samuel. He had been searching many regions for his family's lost donkeys. When all seemed hopeless, his servant suggested they look for the man of God named Samuel, hoping he would help them. Meanwhile, the Lord told Samuel to keep his eyes open for a man from the tribe of Benjamin. Once God pointed him out, Saul was to anoint him as the new leader of Israel.

After they met, Samuel put Saul's heart at ease by letting him know the donkeys had been found. Then he stated God's instruction to tell Saul he would one day be the leader Israel wanted, to bring the people hope. In a position of humility (nothing like during the battle against the Philistines mentioned earlier), Saul told him he was nobody special. He was from the smallest tribe and the least important family of his tribe no less. Why would God want someone like him? Scripture doesn't tell us much about their conversation, but I can imagine them sitting at a fire while Samuel began to tell stories of prophecy. With wide eyes, Saul drank in everything Samuel said and eventually fell asleep to dream about what the fulfillment of those prophecies would look like.

The next morning, Samuel anointed Saul as ruler over Israel. As Saul started to leave, Scripture says God gave him a new heart. "The Spirit of God came powerfully upon Saul, and he ... began to prophesy" (1 Samuel 10:10). The Lord knew Saul would need His Spirit if he were to take on this task of leading Israel. At the time, Saul showed humility and a willing heart, both desired traits in Israel's first king.

We see the Holy Spirit's influence with other Old Testament leaders as well. Joshua showed a heart of humility by staying in the tent after Moses would exit because his hunger for more never allowed him to be satisfied. It should be no surprise to us when God asked Moses to "take Joshua son of Nun, who has the Spirit in him, and lay your hands on him" (Numbers 27:18). Like Joshua, we can choose to live with a softened heart and a willingness to obey. God also brought Othniel to the people, in a time they were crying out for help because of fear. The Lord showed mercy as "the Spirit of the Lord came upon him, and he became Israel's judge" (Judges 3:9-10). His victories resulted in 40 years of peace for the land. We may not be going into a literal war like Othniel, but we can go to war for our house–fighting for a healthy and multiplying culture in our churches. Gideon was also filled with the Spirit to accomplish a God-given task. His willingness to obey came with its challenges, as he learned to be led by truth and not fear. Initially, he was terrified to lead the people, feeling inadequate and unimportant, yet the Spirit filled him and turned him into an incredible leader. Like Gideon, we may feel inadequate, but the Spirit is with us as we lead the people God has entrusted to us.

None of these men lived a perfectly obedient life, walking in a constant state of humility and honor toward the Lord. However, what they did implement for seasons in their life was the choice to listen to God's voice and walk in obedience. We can do the same, but it's even better for us living post-Jesus' resurrection. After His ascension, the Holy Spirit was given to those who would obey Him (Acts 5:32). He descended on the people, giving them the power to be His witnesses around the world. The Holy Spirit doesn't just fill determined leaders, at set times, for specific tasks like in the Old Testament. Today, He is with us. Continually. With Him, we can accomplish the greatest task of all: discipling others and growing God's kingdom. Aren't you glad the empowerment of the Holy Spirit doesn't come and go, but instead is available at any time? I know I am!

Over twenty years ago, a little start-up took their company to the next level and began mailing DVDs as a new and upcoming rental service. I assume with just one little sentence, you already know the name of this company. Founded by Reed Hastings and Marc Randolph back in 1997, Netflix promised better service than its competitors by allowing members to rent up to four movies at once with no preset return dates.[8] It was really quite genius, because who actually returned their rentals on time? (I'm surprised I was even allowed to hold a library card with my inability to turn things in on time.) By 2007, they jumped into the world of streaming, allowing customers to watch an unlimited amount of movies and TV shows for a determined price. It's amazing how quickly technology advanced, where a business model completely changed within ten years of its inception, and it's continued to evolve since then.

---

8 https://en.wikipedia.org/wiki/Netflix

When the Holy Spirit came on the scene in the Old Testament, it was very much like those first ten years of the coveted red envelope. Netflix required a commitment from their customer, and as a result, new envelopes would show up in their mailbox every month. Similarly, God required a commitment from the leaders He would allow the Holy Spirit to descend on. If they were willing, He would come and equip them for the task they'd been given. For a set amount of time, He was present, working through those leaders to accomplish His purpose, and then He'd leave again. It was a come-and-go relationship. Until Jesus returned to heaven after His resurrection, this was the relationship the Holy Spirit had with God's people.

Like Netflix, the relationship between God's Spirit and His people eventually changed. In the New Testament, the Holy Spirit entered the scene, planning to stay for good. For those who showed commitment to Him, as both humble and willing, He decided to stick around for an unlimited amount of time to accomplish the task God had given His church. In fact, that very task given to the disciples over 2,000 years ago still has not changed. We are called to make disciples and to teach them in the way of Jesus. His time with us is unlimited because He is inside us. While our hearts cannot be compared to an entertainment service, it sure makes for a great illustration of how our relationship with the Holy Spirit has evolved since the coming of Jesus. Nevertheless, may we be reminded He was given to those who would obey Him.

The Holy Spirit is not interested in partnering with people who are only willing to put one foot in; He wants to partner with those who are all in–both feet exuberantly jumping into whatever He has in store. Netflix hasn't remained the same since 2007. As you probably know, most recently the company began to crack down on their customer base because they discovered many wanted the convenience of their company without the commitment. They were using their friends and family's log-ins to watch their favorite shows without having to pay the cost. **Our relationship with the Holy Spirit is only beneficial when we are willing to pay a cost.** It begins with a posture of humility. He wants people who are willing to pay in order to receive the benefits–which include boldness, courage, wisdom, and everything else we need in order to make disciples. He will lead us down new avenues, paving new paths we would miss without His guidance. As we humbly follow Him, we show our willingness to go anywhere, do anything, and say whatever needs to be said. When we surrender our own plans, we can trust Him to lead us into what's not just next, but what's best for us and those around us.

Saul started as a humble leader. He would not tolerate unrighteousness and chose to use his kingdom to help fight against it. He knew there was an expectation God had for his people, and he was going to abide by it. Until he didn't. His disobedience in not waiting for Samuel began a slow drift into what later became an arrogant man. His pride led the way as he deteriorated into a vengeful, jealous, insecure leader. Imagine what would have happened if Saul had chosen to open the gate to his heart and allowed God to work in him, and through him, cleaning house as he mended broken places. Opening this gate would have allowed for humility to surface. It would permit the Holy Spirit to flood in and provide for a dry and parched soul.

Thirty miles from my house is the Upper Souris National Wildlife Refuge. This area is a safe place for migratory birds and other wildlife, along with all the plants found in the northern prairie. Within this refuge is an embankment dam called Lake Darling Dam. An embankment dam is just a fancy way of saying it's an artificial one made of plastic, soil, or rock. They are perfect for wider valleys, which is the lay of the land where I live. For us, Lake Darling allows water to be used for conservation and helps with flood control. The prairies and farmland in our region are dependent on dams like Lake Darling because they allow water to be released onto dry farmland and for the growth of hay. Being in the heart of cattle country, we are dependent on hay to feed our livestock. For example, in 2021, North Dakota hit extreme drought numbers, and our farmers and ranchers were desperate for moisture on their desiccated land. Lake Darling Dam released water that year, while not solving all drought complications, and it allowed our farmers and ranchers a chance to limp along until the season ended. Imagine if the dam just held all its water, and no one took the time to release it. Our farmers and ranchers would suffer greatly, along with our local economy. A dam is not made to only hold water; its ability to conserve is for more than creating a big lake. It's intended to preserve water for times like drought when crop growth has not only stagnated but also declined.

Like the reserve, our heart has a dam around it too. Unlike Lake Darling Dam, we do not have someone standing at the gate available to unlock it when it needs to be opened. Instead, when we walk humbly with the Holy Spirit, our position of humility is what will open the dam. We can choose to posture ourselves in a way that allows the gate to unlatch, or we can be like Saul and hold everything so close it's like the gate rusted shut. This is how we hoard the Gospel for ourselves. If the gate doesn't open, the Holy Spirit doesn't flow. If the Holy Spirit doesn't flow, we have to do everything in our own power. And let me tell you, friends, your power–your leadership–just isn't enough.

Before we can walk humbly with the Holy Spirit, we need to truly understand what living humbly even means. As pastors, we often talk about humility because Jesus was the best example of it. But let's be real–the embarrassing stories we share in our messages on Sunday are not evidence of humility. Our willingness to admit when we are wrong, while good and helpful, does not encompass a humble heart. When someone compliments our leadership, and we respond with, "God gets the glory!" isn't a true measurement of whether we lack pride or not. These can often be a source of false humility. We can easily fall into the trap of believing our efforts are what make God proud. Sometimes we are so good at 'faking it till we make it' we lose the true meaning of humility. We are convinced by the lie which tells us our work is what brings our salvation. Unfortunately, our work will always be insufficient.

Humility begins with a genuine response of gratitude. We share from our pulpits all the time about the saving grace of Jesus Christ, but when was the last time we sat in silence as we processed all Jesus really did? Whether you grew up in the church or got saved in prison, we all started in this world as filthy, dirty sinners. There was nothing in our power to make us holy, righteous, clean, or worthy enough to even be permitted to step toward Him, let alone have a relationship with Him. Let's just admit it—without Him, we are a hot mess. But Jesus. Jesus came, and through His death and resurrection, He made us clean. He made us holy, righteous, and worthy. You and I sure didn't deserve it. I'll be the first one to stand up and say I am nowhere near worthy of His love, yet here I stand—deeply loved by the Father. When we become genuinely grateful for what He did, and for the gift of the Holy Spirit, it begins to change everything within us. All of a sudden, we see the world in a new light. It's no longer about those who complained about the worship set choices from last Sunday, or the person who approached you after your sermon stating you "missed it in your message." We are no longer concerned about who likes us and who doesn't, because we don't answer to them—we answer to the one who gave His life for us.

Our gratitude eventually grows into trust. I have been in ministry for over twenty years, and I can tell people 'til I'm blue in the face the importance of trusting Jesus. But when He asks me to trust Him with something unexpected? It's a totally different story, right? I like things a certain way and order, and when they don't go as I planned, I freak out. This kind of freak-out is a definite reminder for me to find some quiet time with the Lord. As I make time, He never fails to remind me who He is. "Sara, are you the one who created the universe? Did you create life with your breath? Did your sacrifice affect eternity for every soul who lives on Earth? No. None of that was you. So why is the One who did such epic feats (that's me, by the way) so hard for you to trust?" By this point, I'm sweating bullets because I know He's right. I am so grateful for what He did, which challenges me to trust Him. I can bring my fears to His feet and let Him take care of whatever makes me afraid. Before we know it, choosing to be honest with the Father allows humility to walk through the door. Humility says, "I can't do this on my own. This is only accomplished through my obedience to God himself." It recognizes that looking more like Jesus every day is integral to being a disciple. If we choose not to heed His voice, we are both sinful and helpless, and we will be unable to fulfill the task He sets before us. When we humbly find ourselves in the presence of the Holy Spirit, He Himself opens the gate and floods right in. He fills us with His power–His power to love, and to lead, well.

Humility based on biblical standards and grounded in the character of God shows us God's nature. This is why He sent Jesus, who chose to serve, and allowed Him to be slaughtered on a tree as He submitted to what the Father wanted. David tells us in Psalms, "The Lord is good and does what is right...He leads the humble in doing right, teaching them his way. The Lord leads with unfailing love and faithfulness all who keep his covenant and obey His demands" (Psalm 25:8-10). Who better to learn humility from than the one who embodies it? He teaches us how to be humble when we choose to obey. Easy peasy, right?

I wish I could say it's easy. We may know a lot of the answers to questions or circumstances people bring to us, but we are still human. Pastors are not superhuman. As we desire to live by the Spirit, we wrestle with obedience like everyone else does.

The apostle Philip is a great example of what it looks like to live in step with the Spirit. He was doing what all believers are expected to do–by traveling to preach the Good News about Jesus. The book of Acts tells us he went to Samaria, where crowds listened intently. They were eager to hear the message and see the signs. The city he was in was filled with joy because of the healings and deliverances that occurred in Jesus' name. As a result, new believers were baptized in the faith and began to learn under Philip. It was an incredible time as God moved mightily through him, and later through Peter and John as well. After a while, an angel of the Lord told

Philip to head south. Having spent enough time in God's presence, he had learned to recognize His voice and walk in obedience. It was on his way when Philip met a eunuch from Ethiopia. This man was returning home from Jerusalem and was sitting in his carriage reading the book of Isaiah out loud. Then, (catch this) the Holy Spirit told Philip, "Go over and walk alongside the carriage." Maybe Philip thought, "What if I look like a creeper?" I know I would've thought so. Thankfully, he obeyed and overheard what the eunuch was reading. He recognized the message, and this is where the magic happened. He asked the man, "Do you understand what you're reading?" I love the eunuch's response: "How can I unless someone instructs me?" The man showed a hunger to understand the meaning of the Scripture; Philip saw the opportunity to share the Good News about Jesus, and he seized it! He even baptized the eunuch in the first body of water they found!

This man's heart turning toward Jesus all started with the Holy Spirit telling Philip to head south on a desert road. He had no idea why. He could've asked God: "Why am I supposed to go that way? What am I going to do once I reach my destination? Do I have everything I need to accomplish the task you've obviously set before me?" Instead of wasting time asking God about all the details, he just did it. The Holy Spirit said, "Go!" and Philip said, "You got it, boss!" He trusted the Lord so much that when the Holy Spirit gave him a directive, he didn't question it. He just did it. As a result, now there is an

Ethiopian man from the first century spending eternity with Christ. Talk about a worthy redirection.

As we walk in step with the Holy Spirit, we begin to look more and more like Jesus. Isaiah prophesied the Spirit of the Lord would rest on the Messiah; He'd be given the spirit of wisdom and understanding, of knowledge and the fear of the Lord. Jesus would delight in walking in obedience. Isn't this what we want? To look more like Jesus–the One who the Spirit of the Lord rested on and was given what He needed when He needed it–to delight in walking in obedience?

In leadership, being led by the Spirit is a double-edged sword. The first edge is what it does for our relationship with God. We draw closer to Him as we learn to be comfortable with the uncomfortable, understanding we are not in control. We have no reason to be scared or nervous because if we are following His lead, we know we're doing the right thing. Many of us went into ministry because God led us there, not because we were confident in our abilities to communicate, lead, and share the Gospel. We all had to grow in these areas through life experiences and practice. Just like when God told me to do something simple, like tell a waitress why I had joy. He knew her much better than I did or ever would; I couldn't go wrong in obeying him. Yet I had to learn God knows the people I interact with way better than I do, and He is trustworthy with His promptings. It took practice (lots of practice). As a leader, there's nothing wrong with admitting you're still learning. Stepping toward Him in this manner allows us to be closer to Him, and look more like Him, every day.

The second edge of the sword is our ability to lead. As a pastor or ministry leader, I recognize how we have a vast variety in our house each week. Between the different religious backgrounds, upbringings, and cultural differences, we have quite a unique family, don't we? When we lead them by example (the first edge), our people begin to see they are called to this mission just as much as their pastor(s). They see you are a follower of Jesus just like them, and we are each learning about our specific role in God's kingdom. When they see that being led by the Spirit isn't weird (cuz who wants to be weird?) and is part of your normal, everyday life, they begin to believe they can live by it as well. They see that God placed them in a specific family, job, neighborhood, and friend group so they can be a light. God didn't place them there to simply raise morality. No! He placed them there to disciple others: the new believer, pre-believer, and the curious. As they live led by the Spirit, they become intentional in their conversations with others as they talk about Christ and sin. God confirms He is trustworthy as He prompts them in sharing and not trusting their own understanding.

Once we recognize our job isn't to save people from their sins, the pressure comes off, and we are able to hear His leading better. Let's admit it: as pastors, we must constantly remind ourselves we are no one's savior. As people come to us with questions and problems, we can easily fall back into believing the lie of someone's salvation is dependent on our leadership. May I just be honest with you? If the world's relationship with the Father was dependent on us–this world would be on fire. We must be mindful of this lie because if we are not, it will negatively affect the world and their view of God. It's hard work leading sheep. With so many different opinions, backgrounds, and personalities, trying to get them all moving in the same direction for the purpose of unity is hard. Why not trust the Holy Spirit to help you lead them as they continue learning what it looks like to be a true disciple of Jesus? The day we meet Jesus face to face, we want to hear, "Well done, good and faithful servant." He gave us people to steward. Are we stewarding them well?

I often tell people my disheartening cruise story. Openly admitting my failure to walk in obedience, being broken in a good way, allows me the opportunity to show people I am still learning like they are. Despite my title as pastor, I am still learning to hear His voice, walk in obedience, and trust His judgment over my own. Sharing the story helps me not fall prey to the lie Saul did–believing my own understanding is good enough. Instead, it's helped me strive to be more like Philip as I walk in obedience to the leading of the Holy Spirit. I don't want to obey the second time I'm given instruction; I want to obey the first time. I want the gate to my heart flung wide open to love God so deeply I desire nothing more on Earth than to please my Heavenly Father–even if it means making sacrifices.

So where are you at, friend? Do you have a cruise story, like I do? Do you have moments in the recesses of your brain where you know without a shadow of a doubt you heard the Holy Spirit and you chose to disobey? Let me encourage you that it's okay. It's over. There's nothing you can do to go back and fix it. What matters now is what you do from here on out. God used mighty men like Joshua, Othniel, and Gideon because they were humble before the Lord; they were hungry for more of Him. They didn't always understand why God wanted to use them, and they often felt unworthy, but God saw something in them that was the perfect fit for the mission they were to be given. God sees something in you too. **Sometimes, He will ask you to do or say hard things.** Don't allow fear to become an excuse like I did on my fateful day cruising the ocean. Wake up each morning and tell Him, "All right, Holy Spirit. It's a new day. Let's do this! Give me eyes to see and ears to hear so I can be led by you today." This has become my new routine since that pivotal day. Because of it, I have been given many opportunities to share Jesus with those who don't yet know Him. In coffee shops, doctor appointments, and school offices, God has helped me disciple others, walking with them as they take steps forward in their journey with Him. God designed you perfectly for the task He has given you as a leader, equipping you with the right gifts and talents because you have something to offer His kingdom. Your purpose on this planet is not to carry the title "pastor;" your purpose is to grow disciples. He gave you the role of pastor because He sees in you the ability to multiply and the capability to teach others to do the same. So take some time today, pause before the Lord, and then serve out His mission–the Holy Spirit will lead the way!

Reflection Questions:

- Can you remember a time you didn't obey the prompting of the Holy Spirit? How did it make you feel?

- What does it look like to allow the Holy Spirit to lead, and not our own understanding? Sometimes, the Holy Spirit will ask you to be transparent with someone. Are you willing to be transparent with others? Why or why not?

CHAPTER SIX

THE LIST

"But we will not boast beyond limits, but will boast
only with regard to the area of influence God assigned to us, to reach even to you."
—*2 Corinthians 10:13, ESV*

A few years ago, I worked part-time for a friend
of mine who owned a local auto mechanic shop.
Working as a service writer, I learned quickly
about all things diagnostics and repairs for pick-ups to
minivans. It was quite the learning curve! Choosing to
get as little grease on my hands as possible, I became a
whiz at the computer instead of under the hood. Being
the first female to work at the shop, I made sure to add a
little feminine touch with some flowers at the front door,
and counters wiped clean by the hour. It didn't take long
for me to learn how uneducated I was in the world of
engines, but now I can tell you the difference between
brake fluid, power steering fluid, and blinker fluid. I'm
kidding. Blinkers don't use fluid. I became aware of this
by my second day on the job. To make it even more in-
teresting, I can now tell you how badly differential fluid
smells and warn you never to fall for the "take a whiff of

this" trick. I was clueless at the start of working there, yet I was very thankful to help my friend out for a season. Working at the shop wasn't a reflection of my love for cars. I worked there because I loved people. Sitting at the front desk, I learned about the lives of our customers as they told me stories about their childhood, their children, and even what size fish they caught the weekend prior. Older gentlemen would often be there waiting for me as I walked in, with a hot cup of joe, treating me like I was just one of the guys. It was truly a joy to work there.

One day, a man came in who appeared to know my boss real well. I didn't recognize him, but after getting a better glimpse of him, I saw his collar. Ah, he was a man of the cloth. Fantastic! Since his face didn't look familiar, I looked forward to meeting another fellow pastor in our community. I quickly finished the repair order I was writing and stepped away from my desk to join their conversation. Not long into the conversation, I realized this man may be in the ministry like me, but he and I had very different priorities. I listened to him as he nitpicked about different ministries and televised productions. The purpose of these influencers was to bring awareness to the life and teachings of Jesus, but he seemed to care more about the most minute details, which didn't change the message of the Gospel at all. Trying to appear interested, I became frustrated with his apparent lack of interest in the lives being changed by them. Not being able to stand silent any longer, I boldly stepped into the conversation and asked him, "Sir, don't you think the purpose of this ministry is to highlight the life-changing power of Jesus? It does not appear the message has been changed or twisted." He looked at me, clearly unsure of where I was going with my question. I continued, "As a pastor, why would you pick apart another ministry just because they didn't do things the way you would do them? Isn't it about souls being saved over you being right?" All I could think of was, "Your love for one another will prove to the world that you are my disciples" (John 13:35). As we say in North Dakota, uffda!

I didn't introduce myself to him that day. To be honest, I didn't care if he knew I was a pastor or if I was just a service writer at a car shop. I felt the heat rising inside me. The last thing I wanted to do was go on a tangent right there in the garage about what a true disciple was and how they should actually be living their lives. That particular conversation became a reminder for me how important it was to choose wisely in how I spoke with others, especially as a leader. The influence we have in and outside of our circles has an impact. It's our choice if we make it a positive or a negative one.

This reminder led me down a road of discovery-learning I had become so well acquainted with having faith conversations with religious people; to attempt one outside of these circumstances felt clunky. I didn't want people to feel like a project, yet I felt my inexperience would lead them to believe they were. I hated admitting it to myself, but it was the reality of where I was. I knew this couldn't be an "earn as many jewels in my crown as I can" endeavor. It would have to be a "give people the opportunity to find the same freedom and hope I found" conviction.

Choosing to be intentional in our everyday lives isn't always as easy and smooth as we'd like it to be. We have to be willing to be honest with ourselves, evaluating our actions and our heart. As I chose to be honest with myself, I soon discovered how being a discipler would stretch me in ways I never anticipated or expected. I thought I'd be a pro from the start. Yet here I was, feeling like a beginner.

In the midst of all of this newfound realization, I knew I needed to be more purposeful. A real gift to me in this season of discovery was when I had the opportunity to have a sit-down with a man I have highly admired for years.

It started with my name being drawn for a gift at a conference Dan and I were attending. I had walked by a global missions booth in the vendor area many times. Sharing the work being done in unreached areas, I was intrigued by all the places and people missionaries were able to live life with every day. The sights, smells, and kind faces drew me to their booth, and it was there I saw the giveaway: a basket filled with books and small gifts from around the globe. I immediately filled out a small slip of paper and continued my way through the vendors before heading back to the event. Little did I know it also came with a sit-down conversation with this very man. Between the books he'd written and the life he's lived on the mission field, I have looked up to him since I was a teenager.

Opening my phone during one of the sessions, I was thrilled to discover that I had won the prize! As I made my way to the booth to pick up my gift basket, I was notified of the other part of my winnings. I couldn't believe it! I was going to meet this man face-to-face?! My legs shook from excitement as I made my way to our meeting spot. Our time together ended up being a beautiful three-hour-long conversation as Dan and I chatted with him about life and ministry. I was a stranger to him, yet he was so gracious to chat with us and hear our story. I shared with him my struggles as a leader and the heart behind wanting to grow both myself and those around me. I desired for us as a church to be better disciplers, but I didn't quite know how to get us moving in the right direction. Before meeting him, we'd discovered shifting an unhealthy established culture was hard work. He challenged us in our conversation by how we saw the world and those who live in it.

As I shared with him, we talked about the heart of the Father and what it takes to position ourselves to mirror Him. The wisdom this man carried had me sitting on the edge of my seat, soaking in every word he shared. I probably looked like a brand new kindergartner who was beyond excited to sit on the classroom rug for their first day of school. As our time came to a close, he told me about a training program called Zumé. An online disciple-making training, it walks people through short, applicable lessons on what the church is, what a disciple is, how to share your story in the midst of God's big story, and more. Looking through all the lessons and principles, it appeared to be very mission-like in nature because most of the lessons were geared toward one-on-one discipleship.

After my time with my new missionary friend, I immediately went online to figure out what this thing called Zumé[9] was. Named after the Greek word for yeast, they model the parable in Matthew 13, which illustrates how God uses ordinary people and resources to make an exponential impact in His Kingdom. Just like a tiny bit of yeast can affect a large batch of dough, we can affect our world for the cause of Christ. Each and every lesson had my full attention. One lesson in particular would forever change my life. It was called the List of 100.

List of 100

	Disciple	Unbeliever	Unknown
1.			
2.			
3.			
4.			
5.			
6.			
7.			
8.			
9.			
10.			

---

9 Curious about Zumé? Head to https://zume.training and see what else the training may have that both you and your church could benefit from.

The List of 100 is a list compiled of people we see on a regular basis–every human we see each week. And I'll tell you what... it wasn't easy to fill out. Of course, I made it pretty hard for myself by not allowing anyone on the list to be from church, not because I didn't want to disciple people in my church, but because I knew I needed to push myself out of my comfort zone. As I began to build the list, I had to process what each week looked like and think of every person I encountered. I thought of the barista I saw every Monday morning during my writing sessions, and my neighbor with his kids who shot hoops down the street every day after school. I thought of my mailman, the grocer, and the sweet lady who greets me every time I walk into Walmart. I began to list them–even if I didn't know their names.

Putting my nose to the grindstone, I wasn't able to fill out all 100 slots initially, but landing in the 80's, I was amazed at how many people I encountered weekly. I labored over the list, yet there was still more to do! After writing down names, I was then required to mark down whether I knew they were a disciple, an unbeliever, or if I was unsure where they stood with Jesus. I ended up with a lot of check marks under the 'unknown' category. This helped me see what my first task would be as a result of this list: get to know the people better. As uncomfortable as it initially made me, it forced me to look at where God had placed me. It propelled me to do my part in making an exponential impact for His Kingdom.

List of 100

	Disciple	Unbeliever	Unknown
1. John's coach	X		
2. Barista at Caribou Coffee		X	
3. Neighbor Susan	X		
4. Neighbor Todd			X
5. Neighbor Mike		X	
6. Neighbor's kid Lucy	X		
7. Neighbor's kid Kia	X		
8. Julie – admin at kids' school			X
9. Corrina at the grocery store			X
10. Kevin at the music store		X	

What did I end up seeing? A lot of people in my life were living without the hope of Christ. I saw people on my list who were following the empty promises of the world, making decisions based on feelings and whims, and wondering why they often felt so alone. And what was I doing to help them? At the moment, nothing.

Admitting I had been positioned in the lives of people to be a witness of Jesus, and was doing nothing about it, was painful. I'd learned over the years how admitting hard truths hurt, but they were rarely the end of the story. As I sat there, staring at my list, I couldn't help but think of Queen Esther. She had been positioned in a place of influence, and after being given wisdom by her cousin Mordecai, she chose to take action. Couldn't I do that too?

As a young Jewish girl turned queen in Persia, Esther found herself in quite a predicament. Her cousin Mordecai, who raised her like his own child, had upset a powerful official named Haman. Haman became so upset with Mordecai that he not only wanted to wipe him from the kingdom, he intended to wipe out his people entirely. Conniving a vicious plan, Haman convinced King Xerxes to make a decree that declared, "...all Jews–young and old, including women and children–must be killed, slaughtered, and annihilated on a single day" (Esther 3:13). When Mordecai heard the news, he was devastated. Choosing to honor God over a haughty official not only put him in hot water but it also put an entire nation of people living in the empire at risk.

Desperately drawing at straws, Mordecai mourned publicly for the future ruin of the Jewish people. Covered in burlap and ashes, he cried bitterly as he walked the streets of Susa. Once Esther heard about Mordecai's behavior, she asked about what troubled him. After a few attempts to reach her cousin, he sent her a copy of the decree made by her husband at the influence of Haman. He asked her to plead for mercy to the king. There was a problem, though: the king had no idea his beautiful bride was Jewish. Regardless of the fears they faced, Mordecai responded in a way that would forever change both Esther's life and the lives of her people. He told her, "Don't think for a moment that because you're in the palace you will escape when all other Jews are killed. If you keep quiet at a time like this, deliverance and relief for the Jews will arise from some other place, but you and your relatives will die. Who knows if perhaps you were made queen for such a time as this?" (Esther 4:13-14). He's telling her, 'Esther—you have been put in a position of influence. Use it, and people will live.'

Gazing at my list of 100, I felt God whisper to me, 'Sara—I have put you in a place of influence by giving you people to interact with weekly. Take advantage of it, and people will live.'

When Dan and I were first married, he jumped into his first full-time ministry job while I toiled at finishing my schooling. During those first few years of marriage, I worked in a local shoe store to help make ends meet. Between figuring out my role as a children's pastor's wife, studying for tests, and writing term papers, my friendships mostly consisted of my shoe-loving co-workers. Every one of them had some kind of church background but, as adults, were no longer participants in any local churches. Adjusting to their adult years, they decided religion was good to have in their back pocket in case of an emergency, but determined it wasn't necessary for their everyday life.

I loved working with this eclectic group of people. We laughed together as we stocked shelves. Busy days ended with high-fives for surviving the crowds and messy aisles. We even attended weddings together. My favorite times, however, were when the store was quiet, and we were able to talk about life. We talked about relationships, past regrets, family dynamics, and, yes, even faith. Halfway through my tenure at the store, I began to notice the questions my manager was asking. I noticed how our faith conversations went from casual to thought-provoking. She wasn't just processing what we talked about in the store–she was also considering them outside of work. Through those conversations, I could see my manager was seeking. She was open to not only sharing her story but also to hearing mine. As she listened, she learned my story was just a small piece of a bigger story–God's story. She carried a lot of hurt from the past and was desperate to be set free from the pain she bore daily. She heard a theme of freedom in the stories I shared: life was hard, yet I was confident God would walk with me through every difficult circumstance.

The late-night shoe store conversations we had eventually led her to a support group. Her support group led her to a life-changing relationship with Jesus. Over time, she uncovered her piece in God's story, finding the freedom her heart craved. Today, she's using what she found to share the Gospel message with others. My other co-workers, however, were not there yet. They were willing to share their stories but not quite ready to listen to mine. It's discouraging when someone isn't ready to listen, but it should never stop us from continuing to try. It is not our job to save–not even as pastors. It's not our job to carry the weight of a super-Christian, where we know everything and make every right decision when it comes to navigating faith conversations with pre-believers. Our job is the same as every other follower of Jesus who desires to live out their call to disciple: to be fishers of people.

Do you ever put yourself in the shoes of people in Scripture and wonder what it would've been like to be in the midst of the stories we love to read? I often wonder what it would have been like to be Peter and Andrew on the day Christ called them to follow Him. After a long night, with nothing to prove for it, they were asked if a teacher could stand in their boat while he continued to instruct a large crowd. Peter sat in his boat with the teacher. He listened intently to his message while probably stewing about having caught nothing from the night before. At the end of his teaching, the teacher had the audacity to say, "Try throwing your net out one more time." There must have been something convincing in the teacher's eyes because, despite their previous efforts, Peter chose to cast the nets anyway. I love to imagine the shock they must have experienced when the boat about tipped over from the weight of nets filled to the brim! Scripture says Peter was awestruck. From this come words that will permanently change their lives: "Don't be afraid! From now on you'll be fishing for people!" (Luke 5:10).

If I were Peter, I would've thought, "Fishing for what?!" I often relate to Peter when I read about him in the New Testament. Like me, he seemed to be more of a black-and-white thinker. I struggle to see things in allegory, and I especially have a hard time grappling with gray areas. I mean, does gray even exist? To be told I would no longer be fishing for fish but instead would be fishing for people–I would be utterly confused. However, as we follow the life of Peter and the other disciples, we begin to see what fishing for people looks like.

As we read through the New Testament, we see the disciples fishing for men in various ways. They would travel and tell everyone they met about the Kingdom of God. They would heal the sick and those with physical ailments and disabilities. They would feed the hungry and help people like the Ethiopian eunuch better understand Scripture and how it relates to the death and resurrection of Jesus. And they would give generously to the poor, all as a platform to share with others about the life-changing power of the one called Christ.

The disciples had one thing in common: their love for Jesus compelled their love of fishing for people. Our role as ministry leaders should not be what compels us to love fishing for people. We can often confuse our title or role as a ministry leader with our relationship with Jesus. However, they are two very separate things. Our relationship with Jesus should be what compels us to love fishing for people. He has placed us in all kinds of circles for one reason: to make Him known. For those in parachurch ministries or who work outside of their church roles, He put you in your workplace for a reason. Additionally, even those working full-time in a church have been positioned in places outside of the church for a reason. He put your kid in a specific class with a specific teacher on purpose. He put you with a particular doctor, your child on a specific sports or academic team, and you in your neighborhood for a reason. It is by no mistake you've been placed where you are because God has given you people He trusts you to steward well.

The disciples were a great example of learning what it looked like to be fishers of people. Even when they had to shake the dust from their feet and move on to share the Gospel with others, it never stopped them from picking up their pole every day and remaining as fishers of men. It reminds me of my friend Ken. Like Peter and Andrew, Ken loves to fish. He spends every waking hour he possibly can over the summer months on the lake. He wants to catch as many fish as his rod will let him because reeling in walleye is incredibly satisfying—mostly because he knows how good they taste. They motivate him to keep casting his rod and jigging for those freshwater beauties.

It's when he catches smelly carp that fishing can be more of a challenge. Bite after bite of these undesirables could convince a guy to give up and head back to shore, yet Ken's love for fishing is too great to let messy fish keep him from casting one more time. When we love the people around us like we love ourselves, even the hardest-to-love people, we are being good stewards of those God has given to us for such a time as this. We are learning to love like Jesus. When we show them His love, we are helping them discover Christ. The question we need to ask ourselves is: "Am I using the influence God has given me to bring my list of people closer to

Christ, or am I choosing to squash it because it's too hard, too scary, or because I've convinced myself I don't have enough time?"

Do you remember writing down your Christmas wishlist as a kid? My children have mastered their wish-list-making skills so well that we now have a shared document where they can add what they want any time they think of something they'd like for their birthday or Christmas. We often have a good chuckle over new items we discover listed. Sometimes they're needs such as socks, a jacket, or even new bedsheets. Other times, they're silly ideas like a butter knife with their name engraved on it, pickles, and even a girlfriend. My youngest doesn't have a phone yet, so with every trip to the store or every commercial he sees on TV, we add to his ever-growing list. Usually consisting of 'larger than my budget can handle' LEGO sets and 'larger than his room can store' sporting equipment, this kid dreams big. He doesn't care how long or short his list is or even if he gets all the items or not. The dreaming, hoping, and game of anticipation is what gets him fired up the most. His grandparents will ask what he would like as a gift, and we laugh. We tell them he will love anything they get him because he loves being entertained by the question, "What if?" Even as a middle schooler, he will bubble with excitement as his birthday draws close because he can't wait to be surprised with whatever he receives. I love his knack for list-making, and I love how easy it is to make him smile.

You and I have a list too. Zumé calls it the List of 100. God calls it your sphere of influence. You may call it the overwhelming call of the Great Commission. No matter what it's called, what if we looked at it from the perspective of my twelve-year-old son? Let's dream big! Let's dream about all those around us who could be living with eternal hope–salvation given by Jesus Christ Himself. Think of how their lives would be changed.

It is no surprise you live in the neighborhood you live in. Yes, you are in the community you live in because God placed you in the church and ministry where you serve. But it's about so much more than that. You live in your neighborhood for a reason. Your neighbor with the unkept gardens, the children playing basketball in the street as the sun goes down, and the elderly man whose wife passed away last year is in your life for a purpose.

It is no surprise you've been put on the community board, whether it's for the park district, public schools, or even for historical preservation. Working alongside people from all walks of life means volumes of stories. These stories are of lives lived to the full, and lives filled with survival at the forefront. Some are cheerful by nature; others take time to warm up before they feel safe to trust. We learn their names, their stories, and why their community matters to them.

It is no surprise that your child was placed on the tennis team they're on. Cheering on students in their youth sports endeavors not only builds community, it allows you to build relationships. Both you and your child have now been given an opportunity to grow close to the other families on the team. Living life together, one season at a time, can be a gift.

Some of the people you see consistently know Christ. Some may have grown up in the church, but they haven't experienced a relationship with Jesus. Others either want nothing to do with the church or have no clue how Jesus' life had significance beyond stories from a dusty old book at their grandmother's house. Are we doing anything about it? Do we even know their names? Have we taken the time to listen to their stories? Have we been their biggest cheerleader and their biggest support? It's not just about being nice and being there for those in our community we see on a regular basis. It's about showing and sharing the love of Christ, so all may hear–and all may know–Him.

Before moving on to the next chapter, grab a piece of paper and a pen. It's time to write down your list. Who's in your circle? Who has God positioned in your life to influence? Write down their names. As we dream and anticipate what could be, let's be intentional fishers of people.

Reflection Questions:

- Did you write out your list of 100? If not, do so now.
- Do you find it hard to list people who are not associated with your church? Why or why not?

CHAPTER SEVEN

THE BUDDY SYSTEM

"As iron sharpens iron,
so a friend sharpens a friend."
—*Proverbs 27:17*

I was an awkward teenager. I mean, weren't we all? Like most teenagers, I had this weird inner dichotomy brewing inside of me. I was desperate for friends, yet was also content with the few I had. I didn't always know how to behave around others, either. However, in my inner circle, I appeared normal. Feeling constantly like a yo-yo, I chose to remain faithfully loyal to a few while allowing others to see my flimsy attempts at friendship-making. When I was seventeen years old, I decided to make my car an art project. Wanting my friends to see how much I treasured our friendship, I allowed them in on my artistic venture. Disastrously, my creative pursuit left me driving a car with a bright yellow trunk covered in handprints. Yeah, that's not awkward at all. I could never quite figure out how to fit in, which caused friends to come and go. I look back now and am thankful for the few close friends I had who still loved me despite my artistic expressions, but in the moment, I remember feeling like I didn't belong.

In High School, I had the opportunity to join my youth group on a missions trip. We joined with other groups from around the state of Minnesota and prepared for a trip to England. I was thrilled to go but terrified of not making friends and feeling alone the entire time. The intent of this mission was to work with local churches as we visited schools during the day and provided services for those same students in the evening. It was on this trip I discovered my ability to talk with complete strangers; I found myself able to introduce myself with such ease to other students at the school, hear their stories, and invite them to the church in the evening, where we played games, sang songs, and shared the message of the Gospel. It was a perfect opportunity for students like myself to see how pulpit ministry often only works when we're also doing ministry away from the pulpit, helping us understand that ministry isn't a glamorous, stage-life profession. Students who just wanted to sing solos or share their testimony would not be nearly as effective as those who built some sort of relationship with a student when we visited their school. If that were the case, the message was simply from a random stranger who carried no influence in the life of a student.

In the middle of the trip, we stopped at a local pub for some lunch. With such a large group, students were coming and going throughout the pub, moving from table to table and chatting with their friends. With a long drive ahead of us, another student and I quickly ran to the restroom before getting back on the bus. Unbeknownst to us, it left while we were washing our hands. Of course, this was in the days before cell phones were widely available, so we had no way to contact anyone about our unfortunate circumstance. Even so, we would've had no idea how to contact the team leaders or the bus driver anyway—we were teenagers who hadn't exactly listened to all the instructions. So, we waited. Wishing once again that people would just notice me, I sat on the front step of this pub, elbows on my knees while my heart beat wildly, hoping someone would notice we were missing and come rescue us.

I learned a valuable lesson that day, and it wasn't being sure I wasn't the last one to use the bathroom. Whenever I am on an overseas trip now, whether I am leading it or participating as part of one, I always make sure some sort of buddy system is used. It was also a lesson my leaders learned while in England because no one wants to be known as the leader who left a student at a pub while in a foreign country. The buddy system helps people have someone to hold them accountable for their whereabouts and the time frame given when exiting the bus. Without this accountability, people could be forgotten if someone fails to keep sight of them.

The buddy system can be used for other things besides travel; it's just coined differently. Also known as accountability, it can be used in many different ways: addiction services, weight loss, schoolwork, and budgeting. For example, my daughter took an online foreign language class during her freshman year of high school. All three of our children attend public school in person, and taking online classes was never on our radar. It wasn't until her high school discovered they weren't able to provide the class she signed up for the previous spring that she learned about the world of online learning post-pandemic. We discovered the state provided plenty of options for high schoolers to supplement where their schools were unable to give instruction, whether it was because of not enough interest or lack of teacher availability. As parents, we were hesitant at first. How in the world would a 14-year-old be able to keep up with an online course successfully, especially when it was in a foreign language? We brought our questions to her school counselor and were presented with their plan of action when it came to accountability for our daughter. She wasn't left to her own devices, hoping she kept up without any support. Between her online teacher, her school counselor, the foreign language department at her school, and her parents, we would all be part of her support system to help her be successful in learning.

This is a simple example, but it reminds us that without having someone in our life to give an account for what we are doing, we can find ourselves facing a fear, a problem, or an issue without even sometimes realizing it. The weekly report we received of our oldest's class progress helped me know if she was on track or if she needed more structured time to focus on her studies. There were a handful of times when I discovered she was falling behind, and when confronted with it, her first response was, "Oh, it's fine!" (like most teenagers would respond, right?). It wasn't until I would sit her down and question why she wasn't able to complete assignments the week prior that she realized she had set herself up for having overdue work because she chose to do other activities instead of making time for her schoolwork. As her support system, we were there to help my daughter find success in her class. We acted as an anchor, doing our best to prevent her from drifting and to keep her on course. The wisdom we've learned over the years when it comes to organization and meeting goals needed to be passed down to her so she could learn those same principles. Paul told the Ephesians, "So be careful how you live. Don't live like fools, but like those who are wise" Ephesians 5:1). We value the support system that comes around her to help hold her accountable, because we don't want her to live like a fool.

While most of us are not taking an online high school course, the buddy system is vital to our life as a believer. Think of it like an open-door policy, where we give an account similar to an income/expense report. All the things addressed in this book up to this point are what's required of those who consider themselves to be followers of Jesus. You, as a leader, especially need to be living in such a way. But if we have no one to hold us accountable, no one to give a report on how we live, we will simply coast our way into a life we never anticipated.

Depending on the denomination, movement, or church you are part of as a pastor or leader, you have someone who oversees you. Maybe you report to a superintendent, administrator, bishop, or pastor in the work you are doing for the church. For my husband and I, we have a regional presbyter we report to, who then reports to a network superintendent, who then reports to a general superintendent. These leaders hold us accountable when it comes to how we pastor our people and operate in the workings of the church. They make sure we handle pastoral care, finances, messages, and ministry with great care. And this is good. We are grateful for them because they keep their sights on us for the greater good of our church. But it is not their responsibility to hold us accountable for our walk with God–how we grow and challenge ourselves as followers of Jesus. We need other people in our life, who we consider trustworthy friends and mentors, to challenge us as leaders in being healthy and leading by example to those we serve.

I remember when Dan and I were first married. We were learning how to maintain our personal relationships with God yet also grow together in the Lord as a couple. Not growing up with a male figure in my home, I was thrilled at the idea of having a man who could hold me accountable in my walk with God. However, when I mentioned this to him, I did not receive the response I had hoped for. In love, he told me it would be a joy to read Scripture and pray together but that it was by no means his job to maintain my relationship with Jesus. It stung when he said that, but it's true. I am responsible for my relationship with Jesus. The same goes for our overseeing leaders. It is not their job to maintain our relationship with Christ. Instead, it is our job to surround ourselves with people who will push us deeper in our walk with God–people who will challenge us to walk in obedience, even if that means walking into the unknown. When we do that, we are automatically building our own buddy system.

A few years ago, our church started a three-year coaching journey with Scott Wilson and the Inner Circle. It's an immersive growth experience to help pastors, their team, and their church maximize their kingdom potential. In other words, they help churches make a greater impact for God's kingdom. Each year, we focus on different areas of our church, our leadership, and the health of the pastors so we can do our best to prevent from drifting away from the greater call of the church and to keep us on course. Scott developed this with a team of leaders after serving as a lead pastor at a church he inherited from his father. The things he learned over the years through system dysfunctions, staffing problems, leadership and management struggles, etc., he wanted to share with others so they could be one step ahead of where he was in the same season of ministry.

The first year there was a lot of focus on the health of the pastor. Dan and I attended a retreat within the first few months where we were asked to reflect on the current status of our church and the current status of ourselves. Answering the questions about the church was fairly easy, but the self-reflection was a whole 'nother story. I had to willingly admit I wasn't as healthy as I thought I was. I had found myself headed down the path of coasting–I was living and leading unintentionally. Scott reminded us how finding things that need change isn't a bad thing when he said, "We shouldn't be surprised when God shows us that we need to change. It's the way of life for anyone who is serious about following Jesus."[10] Through an exercise called Growth Teams, God helped me discover something in my own life in need of change. We were asked to look at eight different areas of our lives, determine if we are growing in each of them, and if we had a trustworthy voice speaking in each area. If we couldn't think of anyone, we needed to find someone and ask if they'd be willing to be a voice of accountability. The areas included my true north (someone you can process everything through, whose voice carries more weight for you than anyone else–like a spouse–because you have shared values and both understand God's heart for your life), counselor, mentor, communication, prayer, financial, truth friends (those friends who will tell the truth, no matter what), and health. See the diagram on the next page:

---

10 Wilson, Scott. Ready, Set, Grow, 10 year anniversary addition. 2022. Page 166.

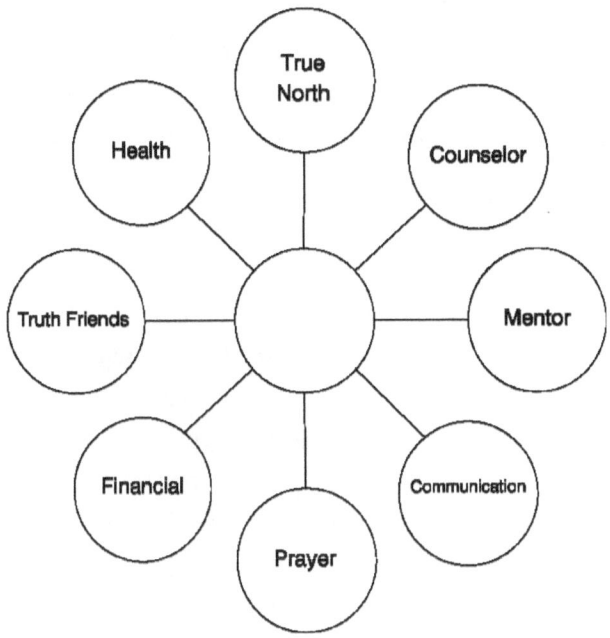

I was able to fill in most areas quite quickly, but the slot for mentor loomed over me for days. It wasn't a heavy cloud, but it left me feeling weighed down because I had no idea who to put in that spot. Staring at the chart for days, I began to pray. "Lord, I don't even know what I'd want in a mentor, let alone who it could be. Help me determine what I want so that it can lead me to who you want."

Reflecting on my life, where I've grown and succeeded, I searched for any gaps that may be keeping me from being as much like Christ as I could be. It didn't take long before I saw a gap I knew needed to be filled. I knew it was something I wanted, and maybe I was already slapping mortar on to begin closing the gap, but I knew I needed someone in my life who could lead and guide me in the right direction. Well, push me in the right direction would be more like it. What was the gap? Discipling people outside of the church. Now listen, friends. I believed in discipleship. I led Bible studies. I hosted small groups in my home. I even taught preschool kids church classes. For years, I did this to help disciple those within the church. Yet, I discovered the lack of one-on-one discipleship in my everyday life. I only discipled when it was "church time." Whether the natural doors of opportunity were not as frequent or just not as obvious, I knew I needed to learn how to look for them and how to open them. Like Craig Groeschel says, "*Unless [I decided] to break the pattern, [my life would] continue moving in the wrong direction. In a circle that never goes anywhere. [Where] it's normal. Easy. The same old rut.*"[11] I needed to break the pattern of using the church as my excuse to disciple, and instead move in the direction of discipleship because I loved Jesus and I loved people. Realizing this, I immediately thought of my friend Kami.

I met Kami at the very beginning of my life in ministry. She and her husband served our network of churches as youth directors, so naturally, my first meeting with her was at a kid's camp. She invited me into her quaint little home, and we sat at her table over tea while sharing our stories. I was drawn to her like a puppy is drawn to a child they know will love them forever. The day we met, I wouldn't have been able to put it into words, but when I look back, I know I was drawn to Kami because she oozed the love of Christ. I knew she would love me well.

11 Groeschel, Craig. Winning the War in Your Mind. 2021. Page 77.

Kami has served God's kingdom in many capacities, from rural American church ministry to across the globe working with unreached people. If there was anyone who could push me to disciple people outside the church, she was the one. I won't lie and tell you it was an easy phone call. I was terrified! This meant I had to admit that even after nearly twenty years of ministry, I still struggled doing the one thing Jesus commissioned us to do—to go and make disciples (emphasis on 'go'). I had to admit I was comfortable in the four walls of my church and rarely bothered to be intentional with my time outside of it in order to reach others with the Gospel. It was embarrassing. I felt ashamed. So before even calling her, I had to get on my knees and ask God to both forgive me and lend me the boldness to step out and 'finally do it already.'

At this point in her life, Kami was doing more discipleship coaching. When I asked her to be my discipleship mentor, she replied with a confident "Yes!" It was the best ask I've ever made. She has been for me what the writer of Hebrews said when he encouraged, "Let us think of ways to motivate one another to acts of love and good works" (Hebrews 10:24). While it hasn't been easy to change my patterns, she has motivated me to love others well and hopefully love them right to the cross.

As pastors, we can be elevated in the minds of others. Whenever I am asked about this, I respond by telling them I actually think it's rather ridiculous! Pastors are normal people, just like everyone else. But, nevertheless, there are those who put pastors on a pedestal, and if we are not careful, we will begin to believe we deserve to be on that pedestal. Without someone to keep us grounded (who can't always be a spouse or family member), we will begin to live, serve, and lead from that place, which will eventually take us down the road of complacency. I don't know about you, but I don't want to be complacent—as a pastor or as a person. I don't want to willingly hoard the best news anyone could hear because I got comfortable. Rather, I want to wake up every morning with a fervent stirring in my spirit, driving me to share the Gospel because I don't want to see others living without the hope of Christ. Accountability stirs that fervency. The buddy system works!

I called Kami because I needed a mentor. However, if you were to ask her why she coaches others to disciple well, I have no doubt in my mind she would say it's because it keeps her on the straight and narrow as well. Hearing other people's stories, and challenging them in how they interact with others, in turn, challenges her. We are walking this road together; it's a mutual relationship.

Mutual relationships help us grow in a variety of ways. I've seen these all take root in my own life once I intentionally asked a few trusted people to hold me accountable to actively sharing Christ with those who were outside of my church.

One of those ways is *it helps shape us.* Just like it says in Proverbs, "As iron sharpens iron, so a friend sharpens a friend" (Proverbs 27:17), a trusted relationship will spur us on to do more for the kingdom. Kami sharpens me. She brings every conversation back to the heart of Christ to remind me I don't do this to please Kami–I do it to please Jesus. She is helping shape me to be more like Christ, and as she sharpens me, I therefore help sharpen her.

When we have someone who is asking the hard questions, it also *helps us grow in wisdom.* Proverbs 15:31 says, "The ear that listens to life-giving reproof will dwell among the wise" (ESV). We can learn wisdom from those who are older than us, but we can also learn from those who are younger than us. All of our experiences have taught us something, and we can take those lessons and share them with others. The buddy system is only successful when it's wanted, so we must be transparent with the lessons we've learned so we can grow in wisdom and, therefore, dwell with the wise like King Solomon tells us.

Sharing this walk as a discipler with others *also edifies us.* In 1 Thessalonians 5, Paul talks with the believers in Thessalonica about the return of Christ. Even though he's aware the believers know the return date is unknown, he reminds them of the importance of being on their guard. As those who live in the light, we are to wear our helmet of salvation with confidence because we know Christ died for us. And then he said, "So encourage each other and build each other up, just as you are already doing" (1 Thessalonians 5:11). Friend, Christ is returning. This is why we disciple others–so that no one is caught off guard. When held accountable, we are encouraged and edified to keep moving forward to not give up this fight against darkness.

The greatest way my mentor relationship has helped me grow, however, has been the fact that *it helps me live with joy and endurance*. King Solomon also told us, "Two people are better off than one, for they can help each other succeed. If one person falls, the other can reach out and help. But someone who falls alone is in real trouble" (Ecclesiastes 4:9-10). Now, I know what you're thinking: this verse is almost exclusively used in weddings. Between you and me, we've probably done thousands of weddings over the years, but let's not look at this verse from this perspective at the moment. Doing ministry is hard work. Being a discipler is hard work. And there are days we feel more like we're surviving rather than thriving. People are messy, exhausting, and sometimes frustrating. But we must endure! Eternity is in the balance. When we have someone walking this road with us, holding us accountable, it helps both of us succeed. If one of us wants to throw in the towel, the other says, "Not yet!" When one of us feels at a loss, the other says, "What about...?"

Determining growth is valuable, Kami and I chose to do our best to chat once a month. In our calls, we talk about life, family, ministry, and even our hobbies. But the meat of our conversation is often centered around one question: "Who are you pouring into as a disciple?" She asks me about the young lady from the chiropractic office, the woman on the farm with her family, the mom who's never prayed out loud for someone before, and the young airmen I had lunch with the week prior. She asks me how I am leading them to the word of God, opening opportunities for them to discover Christ. She challenges me to put my own words, opinions, and expertise to the side and simply listen to their stories–all while praying for God to show me where He's been in their story and to help them see it as well.

Shortly before I started meeting with Kami, I met a young mom named Lainey. She visited our church out of an invitation from an old high school coach. She seemed curious about faith but wasn't ready to commit to attending church quite yet. I saw Lainey periodically, but our conversations often were centered around her children. She was worried their spirited personalities would be too much for those teaching our preschool midweek classes and seemed hesitant to open up out of fear of judgment. I remember one particular day when she had to collect one of her children because of disruptions. I could see both her and her daughters' faces, filled with exhaustion and embarrassment, and my heart broke. Not knowing what else to do, I looked Lainey in the eye and said, "I'm so glad you and your kids came tonight." She politely thanked me, and I didn't see her for months afterward.

Every day, I looked for Lainey–in and outside of the church. I couldn't put my finger on it, but I knew God was working on her heart. Months later, I saw her walk through the doors of our church again, this time with her husband. Still looking unsure, I approached her and asked how she was, beginning a budding relationship. Discovering she had grown up in the church, I assumed once she made the decision to be committed to making church part of her routine again, it would be an easy transition. Boy, was I wrong. This girl had questions, and while she was hungry for more of God, she really didn't know what she was hungry for. She had grown up in church but didn't know Jesus.

Later, I shared with Kami about Lainey and how I had no idea how to help her—I truly felt like I was talking to an unchurched person when I was with her. Having to make another admission, I had to confess I didn't really know how to talk about Jesus with an unchurched person. I had served "church people" for so long that I forgot how to have godly conversations with ungodly people. Because Kami was a trusted person in my growth team, I knew I had nothing to be ashamed of in divulging this new acknowledgment. Happily, she guided me in how to talk with this mom as we talked about the Bible, Jesus, and the hope of salvation. She helped me "work at telling others the Good News, and fully carry out the ministry" God had given me (2 Timothy 4:5). I'm so grateful she did because Lainey's story isn't over. I'll share more about her later.

Her story reminds me of something Matt Walker Thrift shared in his book *Follow*[12]. In response to Prov-

---

12 Thrift, Matt Walker. Follow: Genuine Discipleship in the Modern Age. Self-published, 2024.

erbs 27, where King Solomon talks about iron sharpening iron, he shares a story from his childhood:

"It was a hot humid day in the Maryland summer and the [blacksmith] was wearing a long-sleeved linen shirt covered by a thick leather apron, leather gauntlets, and leather gloves. As sweat dripped from his brow he moved closer to the heat of the forge. Swinging a large hammer repeatedly striking his target, a blob of metal, to create something new from the unassuming raw material in front of him.

I remember thinking about just how uncomfortable this process seemed for everyone and everything involved. The blacksmith was tired and overheated, the hammer seemed to be crying with each calculated connection and the material couldn't possibly be enjoying any part of this.

But through the process, the master craftsman was creating something beautiful, useful, and wholeheartedly different from a block of iron.

I do not believe this proverb [27:17] is telling us that discipleship is easy, but it is absolutely beautiful what God, our master craftsman, can make out of us through the uncomfortability of accountability."

Accountability has taught me it's okay for us to admit we don't know how to do something because it's what motivates us to figure out how to do it. It can be uncomfortable, but through the wisdom and gentle push of others, we can learn how to do things or how to do them differently so others will benefit. God will continue to shape and mold us to be the disciples He wants us to be.

If this hasn't been enough to convince you, let's let the Word of God speak for itself:

"So we must listen very carefully to the truth we have heard, or we may drift away from it. For the message God delivered through angels has always stood firm, and every violation of the law and every act of disobedience was punished. So what makes us think we can escape if we ignore this great salvation that was first announced by the Lord Jesus himself and then delivered to us by those who heard Him speak? [...] Yes, by God's grace, Jesus tasted death for everyone. God, for whom and through whom everything was made, chose to bring many children into glory. And it was only right that he should make Jesus, through his suffering, a perfect leader, fit to bring them into their salvation" (Hebrews 2:1-3, 9-10).

Jesus died for the sake of our salvation. The best thing we can do is lead others like Christ did–leading them straight to the salvation offered by the cross. When we allow ourselves to be transparent with those we've asked to be part of our own buddy system, it keeps us on the straight and narrow. Accountability keeps us from straying because we give certain people permission to call us out and keep us moving toward the path Christ has paved for us. It also allows those in our churches to thrive. As pastors, we cannot hold every person in our church accountable for their evangelistic endeavors; we are not fully responsible for how someone chooses to live their life. We do, however, influence their choices in how we live by the way we live our own lives. When they are given a positive example of accountability, they are able to imitate it themselves. Jesus said, "The gateway to life is very narrow," and the few who remain on that path will be those who choose to be dissatisfied with keeping the news of salvation for themselves. So, let's give them a great example: fighting complacency by being held accountable. Let's allow those we trust to call us out when we become spiritual hoarders ourselves, and choose to live a fervent life as true disciples.

Reflection Questions:

- Who do you have in your life who holds you accountable?

- Have you considered being held accountable for how active you are in sharing the Gospel with those outside your church? Why or why not?

CHAPTER EIGHT

FRANCHISING THE GOSPEL

"You have heard me teach things that have been confirmed by many reliable witnesses. Now teach these truths to others-trustworthy people who will be able to pass them on to others." —2 Timothy 2:2

Growing up in Minnesota, I was surrounded by trees my entire childhood. Enjoying their shade while camping, climbing their limbs when my mother wasn't looking, and collecting all the different shaped leaves was a normal occurrence in my growing years. Moving to North Dakota, however, made me realize how not every landscape is the same. Moving away from the lakes and trees of my beloved home state, I had to come to appreciate the wide open spaces. I've learned how to soak in my time with trees whenever I can. For example, I believe camping should require some trees to sit under while I read a book as my family takes their afternoon naps.

When first moving to our community, I knew I needed to find reasons to fall in love with the landscape and the people. We had left a town I loved dearly, and it was going to take some convincing to believe any city could be as good as what we just left. I truly wanted my heart to be able to do a deep dive into our new environment with no hesitations. We moved just after school had finished, which made meeting new people outside of church and school a challenge. In an attempt to take the bull by its horns, I took the kids every week to a new park in hopes of learning the city's layout better. Maybe we would even meet a new friend while we were there. During our daily adventures, I discovered one park in particular. I fell in love with it because it carried the story of our community and its people with great pride, something I wanted to do. Even though I barely knew anyone in this new place, I felt at peace sitting under the large oak and pine trees.

It may not surprise some of you, but just like people, North Dakota is a little sparse when it comes to trees. We have miles upon miles of prairie, ideal for grazing cattle and growing fields of corn, flax, and canola. Between the wind and the cold temperatures, though, it takes a hardy tree to survive the temperature fluctuations of our hardy little state.

The Bur Oak is a tree that can survive in some of the coldest of winters. While impressive in size, it grows quite slowly. With a lifespan much lengthier than the average oak tree, it can live up to 400 years. Too large to be on most home properties, it's the perfect tree for someone to enjoy its cool shade at their newfound favorite park. In North Dakota, the Bur Oak can grow as tall as 85 feet tall, with a canopy as wide as 60 feet. How lovely it would be to sit under its protection on a hot summer afternoon!

I've planted a few trees over the years and have come to realize I take for granted the large, wide canopied trees in local city and state parks. Those trees were planted years before I was even a thought in my mother's mind, and yet today, I am able to enjoy their shelter. Whether they were planted by a forester or were dropped acorns in nature, we get to enjoy the literal fruit from years before our existence.

The Bur Oak, in particular, begins to drop acorns in nature around their 35th birthday. Once it becomes mature enough to reproduce, it gives back to its environment as a thank-you. Shortly after the tree flowers, the fruiting process of growing acorns begins. Throughout the summer and even into the fall, these acorns begin to grow. Once they become heavy enough, the seeds begin to fall to the ground during late fall and winter. The oak drops these little 1.5" acorns to the ground with hopes of new life coming forth. The tree doesn't want to be barren; it wants to produce. Unfortunately, unless the seed lands in a favorable environment, it has little hope of growing past its seed stage.

The acorn is a heavy seed with a hard exterior, and instead of being carried by the wind, it often falls straight down from the oak's branches. Landing in spaces with no sunlight and harder soil due to the tree's roots, it's unlikely for the fruit to sprout. In addition to the lack of sun and loose soil, animals like squirrels, deer, and rodents traipse through the fallen seeds, collecting and hoarding them for the winter months. It's only when they are left alone, in favorable conditions, that they will eventually become a sapling.

The oak tree gives its acorns everything they need to grow to ensure its stately parent's ability to give life. It's another reminder that healthy things multiply. If an oak isn't producing acorns, a forester would worry about its viability. If a tree isn't producing, it's either dead or dying. This doesn't just apply to the Plantae kingdom; it also applies to the Kingdom of God. If the church isn't multiplying itself, it is either dead or dying. Jesus is clear in His expectation of His followers to multiply. We have people in our churches who have everything they need, but unless they are in the right environment, they will stay hidden within their shells, just like the seed inside an acorn. When multiplication is not encouraged in our churches, there's no movement—no growth. And in God's Kingdom, it's a serious thing not to bear fruit.

Jesus expects His followers to produce fruit. Sharing parables with His disciples, He addressed the importance of producing more than once. In one He shared, "A man planted a fig tree in his garden and came again and again to see if there was any fruit on it, but he was always disappointed. Finally, he said to his gardener, 'I've waited three years, and there hasn't been a single fig! Cut it down. It's just taking up space in the garden.' The gardener answered, 'Sir, give it one more chance. Leave it another year, and I'll give it special attention and plenty of fertilizer. If we get figs next year, fine. If not, then you can cut it down.'" (Luke 13:6-9).

This parable was originally shared as a way to warn the listeners of God's desire to see the fruit of repentance. The listeners had walked away from true faith and the living God, and exchanged it for a works-righteousness. Instead of showing the fruit of repentance, they showed the fruit of self-righteousness. Whether we like to admit it or not, God's patience does have a limit. If we are not living out the great commission as a true follower of Jesus, He has His ax set and ready to swing. For lack of better words, we are of little use to His kingdom if we are not multiplying.

Jesus also addressed how fruit bears witness to the character of a person during the Sermon on the Mount. He explained how one can have no fruit, good fruit, or even bad fruit. He told His disciples, "You can identify [false prophets] by their fruit, that is, by the way they act. Can you pick grapes from thornbushes, or figs from thistles? A good tree produces good fruit, and a bad tree produces bad fruit. A good tree can't produce bad fruit, and a bad tree can't produce good fruit. So every tree that does not produce good fruit is chopped down and thrown into the fire. Yes, just as you can identify a tree by its fruit, so you can identify people by their actions" (Matthew 7:16-20). **It is expected that followers of Jesus produce fruit—good fruit.** What is that fruit? More followers of Jesus.

Jesus told Simon and Andrew to follow Him and that He would teach them to be fishers of men. It's the same for us. He will work in us–showing us the how–so He can empower us to fish for people. When we are truly following Him, growing in godly character, sharing the Gospel, and teaching others to obey God's commands, it shows evidence of the fruit we bear. The problem we have is that many people sitting in our churches on Sunday are not yielding this kind of fruit. They may be producing others, such as kindness, gentleness, or even self-control, but they are not actively sharing the Gospel and raising up more disciples. They may even be inviting friends to church, or inviting them to a small group, but purposeful conversations centered on faith are not happening outside of those spaces.

Why is this so important? Because when disciples multiply themselves, it creates a larger yield than addition. When one person actively disciples another, the Kingdom of God increases by one. As they come to understand Jesus' sacrifice made on the cross, it brings life transformation. From that transformation, they can now live in the hope only Jesus can give them. Yay! What an incredible thing! But it should never end there. The last thing I want to do is downplay someone's salvation experience. Every person who comes to know Christ is worth celebrating. Imagine what our churches would look like, however, if every person sitting in our seats on a Sunday morning were intentionally discipling someone as a result of being discipled themselves. The Kingdom of God wouldn't just increase by one; it would increase by an indefinite number. It's as simple as second grade mathematics: multiplication increases numbers at an exponential rate compared to addition. See below.

| 1+1=2 | 2+1=3 | 3+1=4 | 4+1=5 | 5+1=6 |
| 1+1=2 | 2+2=4 | 4+4=8 | 8+8=16 | 16+16=32 |

If we choose to grow the church by addition, we will never keep up with the population growth of the globe. If we can never keep up with the population growth of the globe, millions of people will die and go to hell because they were never given the chance to hear the hope-filled words of the Gospel. Maybe we can't share the Gospel with the entire Earth from our own little (or big) churches, but what we can do is share with our community. From there, our community can share with our county. Our county can share with our state. Our state can share with our region. And our region can share with our country. It is possible. This is not a far-fetched theory. It's as simple as mathematics.

This is where a culture shift is important. Many feel if the pastor and lay leaders are sharing the Gospel well from their pulpits and places of position, the church will grow sufficiently. This is why people often share the Gospel by only inviting them to church. If they can get them to church, then they can hear about Jesus. This does, indeed, help the church grow, but we unfortunately still have the rest of the body who is sitting idle. If every person who sits in our churches on Sundays were intentionally pouring into someone with the Gospel message, we wouldn't grow by just two or three—we would grow by tens, hundreds, and even thousands.

Subway is my middle child's favorite restaurant. When traveling in the summer for baseball, we cannot play in a town without him suggesting his favorite sandwich as an option after the game. Who cares if we have stuff packed in a cooler in the back of the car? This kid will fight for his oven-roasted chicken on Italian bread. The fact that Subway is basically in every small North Dakota town is definitely in his favor, and while we don't let him win the battle often, we will every now and then let him indulge in a sandwich loaded with lettuce, tomatoes, onions, ranch, and extra jalapeños. Yeah, I know. Gross.

Believe it or not, Subway has roughly 6,000 more locations than McDonalds in the entire country. In August 1965, Subway first opened its doors in Bridgeport, Connecticut. The restaurant was born when 17-year-old Fred DeLuca and family friend Dr. Peter Buck set out to find a way for Fred to pay for his college tuition. Within nine years, Subway multiplied itself into 32 locations all throughout Connecticut. Once Fred and Peter opened the opportunity for others to franchise their restaurant, they grew exponentially.[13]

When a business chooses to franchise, it benefits them in multiple ways. A few of those are faster expansion, shared investment, drawing out ambitious and mo-

13 https://www.subway.com/en-us/aboutus/history

tivated entrepreneurs, and brand recognition. Businesses will grow in size and in the number of locations when
an investor takes the time to train and put boots to the
ground. The brand will grow, it will draw new investors,
and the owner will benefit both in business recognition
and in their financial investment. From one little sub-
marine sandwich shop in Bridgeport, to 32 locations in
Connecticut, to now over 37,000 in over 10 countries,
Subway is living proof of the rapid growth that can be
produced by multiplication.

With its accessibility, our family has often taken advantage of Subways littered around the state. With 65
options available to us, we know there's always a backup
plan if we forget the cooler. If Fred and Peter had chosen
to only open as many restaurants as they were able to,
with the time and resources they possessed personally,
my son may have never been given the opportunity to
eat one of their fresh-fit classics.

There are people in our communities who may have
heard the name of Jesus, but really, they know nothing
about Him. They haven't heard the stories of His mir-
acles, nor have they experienced His divine character
through His love and kindness. It is unlikely for me to
reach all 50,000 people in my area with the Gospel. Yet if
I look at it from a franchising perspective, where I know
if I choose to live a life of multiplication, God's message
will spread faster; there will be more people invested in
the Kingdom of God, it will draw out godly ambition, and
it will make His name more widely known. As a leader, I
must choose to empower others to share the message

by creating a culture of multiplication within my church so that together we can reach our community, watching spiritual appetites devour God's word like a teenager devouring a foot-long in five minutes flat.

I must admit, growing up in the church, I thought I understood the message of the Gospel. Jesus saves, right? However, I would walk the halls of my high school, judging those around me for the things they did wrong. Knowing God called me to be holy, I disassociated with anyone who lived unrighteously because I didn't want to be tempted to live such a life. Without even knowing it, in my attempt to love Jesus, I was willingly choosing not to love those around me.

Eventually, I grew up, went to college, got married, and entered the ministry. I thought I knew what was required of anyone who chose to follow Jesus. I talked about Him a lot with classmates, co-workers, and neighbors. I would pray for opportunities to talk about Jesus, but unless those opportunities presented themselves in a very obvious manner, I chalked it up to how "It wasn't the right time." It wasn't until years later that I began to hear about a pattern of multiplication when I sat down with missionary friends over a meal or hot cup of coffee. I would listen to their stories of the countries and people they served in hard-to-reach places. They would share about picnics, dinners, reading groups, tea times, and holidays–risking their livelihood to share the Good News with others. As I listened, I thought to myself, "I wish I had such opportunities." The gatherings my friends had were to create intentional spaces for faith conversations. It was so much more than relational evangelism. They weren't building relationships solely for the purpose of conversion; it was out of love for a people group they deeply cared for. They wanted to witness people finding hope in Christ, and to equip them to share Christ with their friends and family as well. This caused me to ask myself, "Do I care enough about the eternity of my friends and family to the point I would create intentional spaces for faith conversations? Or am I hoping on a whim that something will be said, or questions will be asked giving me the opportunity to share?" It wasn't about my willingness to share. It was about my willingness to be intentional.

As ministry leaders, we want our team to be intentional when they meet with volunteers. Whether it's equipping preschool leaders or raising worship team members, it's an expectation that they are intentional with the time they have in raising up others. Naturally, then, we should be expecting them to be intentional in finding and raising up new disciples as well. The principles are the same, whether you are developing a new team member or investing in a new disciple. You do it not for your own benefit but for theirs. It's not so our church can grow but so God's kingdom can grow. But why stop there? Our church isn't just filled with our staff and their lead teams; our church is filled with many more people who either claim to follow Christ or are curious enough about faith that they continue to come week after week.

Jesus has an expectation for all who claim to follow Him: to make disciples.

For my missionary friends, making disciples may look different. Depending on the country they serve in, they need to be careful with how they handle faith conversations. As they quietly discuss stories of Jesus from the New Testament, they have to always be aware of who can hear their conversation. If it's not handled with care, they could cause undue harm to their international friends, whether that be excommunication, bodily harm, or even death. Yet one thing remains: those who choose to follow Christ have determined He is worth the risk. As missionaries choose to seek after the one, they raise others up to not only be a disciple but to be a disciple-maker.

How much easier we have it! I can talk about Jesus in the middle of a local coffee shop without a care in the world. It wasn't until after hearing the stories from my friends that I realized how I often chose to be unintentional with my relationships. I allowed opportunity after opportunity to slip by. Sure, maybe I would've dealt with some rejection, ridicule, or even loss, but it wouldn't compare to the stories of others who've lost so much more for the sake of the Gospel. I didn't really understand the role of a disciple like I thought I did. Not until I learned from my global working colleagues, who challenged me to rise to the call God had on me, not just as a pastor but as a follower of Christ.

We must understand that multiplication isn't just about producing seeds that will hopefully bear fruit; it's about caring for the seeds as they grow and mature. Hearing the Gospel message may bring someone to repentance, but it's living life with other believers that help them grow and become believers with strong faith, convictions, and a desire to spread the message themselves. The Bur Oak doesn't just drop acorns, leaving them for squirrels to hoard or kids to throw at targets. Their desire is to allow the seeds to keep the cycle of tree life going.

Interestingly, the Bur Oak has learned to adapt to the cold temperatures up here in North Dakota by dropping its acorns in the fall and not allowing them to germinate until spring. During the long and cold winter (I would emphasize just how long and cold, but my goal is to encourage you to explore the beauty of North Dakota, not avoid it), the seeds require cold stratification in order to germinate. The winter months are too cold for them to survive, so they sit and wait–knowing fertile, rich, moist soil awaits them in the spring. We may not be like magnificently tall standing oaks, who sway in the wind while providing shade for others, but like them, we are beings created by God to multiply. We can learn three things from the grand Bur Oak tree that will help us be the multipliers that God designed us to be.

The first is we must understand that *multiplication is an investment*. The Bur Oak chooses to invest in its seed when it drops, waits, and germinates over seasons. It takes time. Our culture doesn't like that word: time. We are always on the go, never wanting to stop and wait. However, we must choose to commit to seasons of work, investing time and resources. We cannot expect the people in our church to embody such an undertaking if we ourselves are not willing.

Jesus shared a parable with his disciples about the expectations He set for His followers when it came to investing. Using the story of the three servants who received talents when their master went away, He told them it was His choice how much they received. It's also up to the receiver to take what they've been given and multiply it. When it is not multiplied, there are consequences, and what they've been given will be handed to someone else.

We have been given an incredible message. The people in our churches have been given an incredible message. However, if we hoard this message for ourselves, we will be called wicked and lazy servants, just like the man in the parable. "Then the servant with the one bag of silver came and said, 'Master, I knew you were a harsh man, harvesting crops you didn't plant and gathering crops you didn't cultivate. I was afraid I would lose your money, so I hid it in the earth. Look, here is your money back.' But the master replied, 'You wicked and lazy servant! If you knew I harvested crops I didn't plant and gathered crops I didn't cultivate, why didn't you deposit my money in the bank? At least I could have gotten some interest on it.' Then he ordered, 'Take the money from this servant, and give it to the one with the ten bags of silver. To those who use well what they are given, even more will be given, and they will have an abundance. But from those who do nothing, even what little they have will be taken away.' (Matthew 25:24-29).

Those who took the time to invest not only received kind words from their master, but were also trusted with more. They were given the privilege of participating in his success. Our investment should be so much more than sermon prep, Sunday morning gatherings, and group-setting discipleship. These are good; please don't hear me wrong. But we cannot deny the value in an investment of 'the one'--learning someone's name, sitting across the table from them, hearing their story, and sharing with them how we've been changed because of God's story. It's taking time out of our busy schedules, even if it's considered an inconvenience, to infuse the love of Christ in one-on-one conversations is an investment worth making.

The Bur Oak also teaches us the importance of *setting the tone* and establishing a culture of anticipation. It gives every one of its acorns everything they need to become a tall oak inside its hard little shell. When we take the time to invest in someone as we share the Gospel, we are teaching them how followers of Christ have been given everything they need to multiply as well. Creating a culture of multiplication isn't just saying, "Now go share the Good News with someone else" to our congregations. It's choosing to set the tone, bringing a mutual understanding of what God expects from us and what He's given us to meet that expectation.

Peter tells us, "God has given us everything we need for living a godly life. We have received all of this by coming to know him, the one who called us to himself by means of his marvelous glory and excellence. And because of his glory and excellence, he has given us great and precious promises. These are the promises that enable you to share His divine nature and escape the world's corruption caused by human desires. In view of all this, make every effort to respond to God's promises" (2 Peter 1:3-5). Doesn't that sound amazing? The one who embodies marvelous glory and excellence has given us everything we need to share with others about His great and precious promises. This isn't a burden. It's a gift. And as leaders, we get to participate in this gift with everyone God has entrusted in our care as we lead and shepherd them in the ways of Jesus.

Thirdly, as leaders, we not only lead by example in how we invest in others and set a tone of expectation, we also *release those we've invested in,* in order for them to reproduce. The acorns that rested over the winter are preparing for spring. Sitting dormant inside their hard exterior, they anticipate a warm and moist environment come spring so they can do what they were created to do.

Every day, we meet people in our communities who are just waiting for someone to take notice of them—to show kindness, and purposely take the time to get to know them. Our churches must become a suitable environment for seeds to fall. We need to take the time to invest in others, to establish a healthy culture and expectations, and to be leaders who are living proof. It's so much more than teaching Bible stories. People are waiting for someone to say, "You are worth investing in." Choosing not to hoard our time, like the squirrel does with acorns, when we are intentional with our time and allow those we invest in to find their way to fertile ground, they will one day be ready to germinate, grow, and eventually produce. Peter even says, "The more you grow like this, the more productive and useful you will be in your knowledge of our Lord Jesus Christ. [...] work hard to prove that you really are among those God has called and chosen. Do these things, and you will never fall away. Then God will give you a grand entrance into the eternal Kingdom of our Lord and Savior Jesus Christ" (2 Peter 1:8-11).

Contrary to what we may feel, releasing a new follower of Christ to multiply themselves is not like releasing a captive animal back into the wild. They may trip, stub their toe, or get distracted, but just like Peter said, they have been given everything they need to live a godly life. The Holy Spirit came to Earth after Jesus' resurrection for a reason: to teach and guide believers in the way they should go. We must trust that as God transforms them from the inside out, what overflows from that is both beneficial and beautiful.

Growing takes time. God isn't in a hurry because He is knowledgeable of all time–both present and future. And growing takes work. It takes intentionality, stretching of muscles, and a desire to keep taking one step at a time. When the two are combined, we are given the privilege to see God do what He does best: grow His kingdom into something magnificent... through us.

Reflection Questions:

- What kind of fruit are you producing? How about your church or ministry?

- Is your church a suitable environment for seeds to grow?

- Are you prepared to release others to share the Good News?

CHAPTER NINE

EQUIPPING FOR DISCOVERY

"For I am not ashamed of the Good News about Christ. It is the power of God at work, saving every-one who believes." —*Romans 1:16*

Sitting across the table from my friend, drinking my steaming hot almond latte, we caught up on life, work, and all things fall. The weather was beginning to turn, and we couldn't wait to pull out all our sweaters and cozy socks. Once our conversation hit a healthy lull, we opened up the Bible app on our phones and began to read from the book of Genesis together.

"The serpent was the shrewdest of all the wild an-imals the Lord God had made. One day he asked the woman, "Did God really say you must not eat the fruit from any of the trees in the garden?"

"Of course we may eat fruit from the trees in the gar-den," the woman replied. "It's only the fruit from the tree in the middle of the garden that we are not allowed to eat. God said, "You must not eat it or even touch it; if you do, you will die."

"You won't die!" the serpent replied to the woman. "God knows that your eyes will be opened as soon as you eat it, and you will be like God, knowing both good and evil."

The woman was convinced. She saw that the tree was beautiful and its fruit looked delicious, and she wanted the wisdom it would give her. So she took some of the fruit and ate it. Then she gave some to her husband, who was with her, and he ate it too" (Genesis 3:1-6).

As we read through the story of Adam and Eve's act of disobedience, we looked at what the passage told us about God's character and what it told us about our own character. We found ourselves having a lively discussion about the entrance of sin into the world. My friend was very new in their faith and peppered me with questions. "Why did God even put the tree in the garden? Why did they listen to the serpent and not trust God? If they hadn't done it, would someone else have sinned, and we'd be dealing with the consequences anyway?" I loved our conversation, even if many of my answers were, "I don't know." It definitely challenged both of us to look deeper into the text, and to not be satisfied with the surface-level reading.

My favorite question came when my friend asked, "What are the consequences of my sin? Adam and Eve got kicked out of the garden, but what happens to me?" It was my favorite question because it allowed us to talk about the reality of hell. Up to this point, my friend knew God had given them salvation by giving them hope and purpose. But the reality of hell had not been discussed, and it really began to challenge their way of thinking. We talked about how our sin separates us from God, and if we remain separated from Him until our death, it means separation for eternity. Thankfully, because of Jesus' death and resurrection, when we accept Him as our Lord and Savior, we can be redeemed and once again become right with God–causing us to no longer be separated from Him. I watched as my friend visibly let out a deep breath of relief. Thank you Jesus for salvation!

I assumed the conversation would shift from there, but my friend hesitated. Looking me square in the eye, they asked, "What if other people don't know about this? What if they don't know they're not right with God?" The Holy Spirit nudged me as I responded, "Well... it's our job to tell them."

"Wait. It's *our* job? We have to tell them?" my friend asked.

"Yup."

I quickly flipped to the Gospels and read, "Jesus came and told his disciples, "I have been given all authority in heaven and on earth. Therefore, go and make disciples of all nations, baptizing them in the name of the Father and the Son and the Holy Spirit. Teach these new disciples to obey all the commands I have given you..." (Matthew 28:18-20).

Telling my friend that God commissioned His disciples to tell others about Him and to teach them how to obey Him, I reminded them it was now on us. These disciples have come and gone, along with many others who've passed on the message. If it hadn't been for them, we wouldn't be in the position we are today. Now, the baton has been passed on to us, and it is our job to tell others so they are not caught unaware.

My husband grew up with apple trees in his backyard. Every summer, it was the kids' job to pick up the ripened apples off the trees, as well as the rotting ones sitting beneath their branches. He often tells our boys how apple picking is what helped him learn how to handle a hockey stick so well. Every time he and his brother had to go out and pick up the rotting apples, instead of grabbing them with gloved hands, they would set a trash can on its side and shoot the apples in. Their skills were especially needed after a storm when apples dropped by the bucket full. I assume more apple chunks found their way into the grass than they did into the garbage can, but it worked to occupy two very busy boys.

If their family experienced a late frost in the spring, it usually meant a much smaller yield of apple blossoms. I'm not sure if this was a desired outcome for the apple slap shooting, but it hurt the trees' crop and their family's ability to enjoy a plethora of apple butter, juice, pie, and crisp all fall long. It didn't just affect the tree; it affected the family. My friend learned over coffee how a believer's lack of sharing not only hurts the Kingdom of God, it affects the eternity of others. Adam and Eve were separated from God in the garden; we don't want our friends and family separated from Him for eternity. We don't hoard the best news for ourselves; we share it with everyone around us. This rings true for new believers like my friend, as well as seasoned believers who are now in full-time ministry like myself. We share today as if we have no tomorrow.

I remember back when I was fifteen years old. I had been given the opportunity to become a violin instructor. Playing for four years up to that point, my teacher saw potential in me as a tutor. I remember wanting to be an instructor when I grew older, like I saw other classmates of mine did, but I knew I wasn't nearly as good of a player as they were. I watched as they invested hours into their practice time after school. I knew they invested even more time once they reached the threshold of their homes. Listening to them play in the practice rooms, I knew their talent far surpassed my own. There was no comparison.

Many of my classmates started playing at very young ages, as early as four years old. I only started playing the violin when I was an unsure eleven-year-old. I grew up around bluegrass and country music, and playing the fiddle always looked fun to me. I spoke with my orchestra teacher, and he suggested that I initially learn how to play classically. There were some skills that would be hard to gain if I chose to fiddle first. I remember walking into the music store in my hometown, filled with wonder at the two-story-high walls filled with instruments. Holding my rental violin in the store for the first time felt magical. I had no idea how to use it or even how to care for it, but it felt like such a gift to possess one. Bringing it home, I set it in a safe place away from my little sister's hands. Carrying it daily to and from school, I treasured this instrument. However, after a few lessons, I was terrified to ever play my instrument in front of anyone. Afraid of failing, I preferred to hide rather than risk messing something up with eyewitnesses. Instead, I would pull it out behind closed doors at home. At school, I would find an empty practice room out of earshot of anyone. Even when asked to play for my teacher, I nervously looked around the room to see who would hear me play. I allowed my fear of imperfection to drive me. In a group setting, I had no problem playing and allowing my gifts to shine. But alone? Yeah, that wasn't going to happen.

This carried on with me into my high school years, and as a sophomore in high school, I had a dilemma to face. Not even knowing what my teacher saw in me, I had to choose if I was willing to trust his instincts about me or walk away from the opportunity. I also had to face the question of whether or not I would be willing to play in front of others in order to help them grow in their own skill. What if I wasn't good enough? What if I taught them the wrong technique, or my music theory wasn't up to snuff? What if I didn't move my students along at an expected pace? What if they didn't like me, or I disappointed my own teacher? The fear consumed me until my mom intervened, telling me I needed to discuss it with my instructor.

I remember it like it was yesterday. We stood inside his window-encased office, surrounded by instruments, filing cabinets filled with music scores, and a desk piled high with papers, tuners, and rosin blocks. I told him about how afraid I was of failing and that I wasn't sure I was ready to be a teacher for younger children. He looked me in the eye and said, "Sara, I'm fully confident you can lead a student to the next level. All you need to be is one step ahead of them." Of course, I worried about them leapfrogging me, but he assured me it wasn't a concern of his. Reluctantly, I stepped into the world of teaching and learned all I had to do was walk my students through the things I did as a beginner. I leaned on what my instructor told me and did exactly what he did with me when I was a shy and quiet eleven-year-old holding my violin for the first time.

As an adult, I look back and see the risk he took in allowing a fifteen-year-old to teach younger students. From my own life experiences, I've seen how teenagers can be idle if not held accountable. They can also assume an answer without first investigating for the answer. Yet he saw potential in me that was worth the risk. As ministry leaders, we can also take a risk when allowing new disciples to disciple others. There's a chance they may slip up, choose to shy away from hard questions, or even assume answers without digging into God's word to find the answer first. As much of a risk as it is, if we discipled them in a way that can be reproduced, we have to trust the process. My violin instructor taught me in a way I could easily imitate with a student younger than me. He knew I had paid close enough attention in my early years and, therefore, trusted my ability to duplicate all I had learned.

Duplication is the key. But let's be honest: the worry or fear we have in releasing new believers may not be whether or not they're ready. Rather, we may be more concerned with whether or not we prepared them well enough for the task. Is it possible we end up fighting a mindset we created as a result of our own training? If we want to see any form of duplication, we must be willing to see how equipping someone to be a discipler doesn't need a long list of requirements to accompany it. It simply requires one thing: to know and follow Jesus. So, how do we help them become a multiplier? By giving them an example to follow and duplicate.

When my mentor Kami walked me through discipling someone with little to no knowledge of the Bible, the one thing she continued to pound into me was the importance of allowing someone to discover Jesus for themselves. Like a music instructor, I could give them the tools they needed, but they had to be the ones to play the music. My students had to bring their bow to the strings and practice, practice, practice. As an instructor, I could play alongside them, but I certainly couldn't perform for them at their recitals. The same is true when we disciple someone. We could sit and talk about life with them, read Scripture, and even pray with them, but allowing space for them to discover the character of Jesus on their own is of the utmost importance. If we just spewed out all the answers to every question they had, or when we didn't know the answers, to research them on our own, we would not be discipling them in a way that could be duplicated. The goal isn't just to bring someone to the knowledge of Christ; it's also to raise up a disciple who will do the same. When we invest in someone's faith journey, it must be in a way that can be replicated.

Remember Lainey, the young mom I mentioned earlier? When I met her for lunch one day, she asked me if I could mentor her. Filled with so many questions and wanting to learn more about the Bible, she wanted someone to teach her what a relationship with God looked like. As someone who grew up in the church, I was astonished by some of her questions: "Is Joseph, Jesus' dad, the same Joseph we read from in the book of Genesis?" "I know about the Trinity, but who is the Holy Spirit?" "What does the fear of God mean?" and "What are the Gospels?" How did this girl know so little yet was exposed to church her whole life?

My first instinct was to answer all of her questions. However, Kami continued to remind me of the importance of leading my new friend in discovery to find the answers herself. Instead of spouting out the answers to her, we would open the Bible and read together about the stories of Joseph, the references to the Holy Spirit, and when men and women showed the fear of God. Even though Lainey was still learning, and hadn't come to an understanding of her need to accept Christ as both her Lord and Savior, I wanted to disciple her in a way she could duplicate once she stepped into that relationship with Jesus.

Every month, we'd have lunch together. Whether it was over McDonald's or Indian food, we talked about the goodness of God, how both His character and our own are reflected in the Scriptures we read together, and we'd pray. Watching her grow in hunger and understanding was so much fun! Thinking about it now still makes me smile from ear to ear.

My favorite lunch date with her was the day Lainey told me she'd accepted Christ. She had been attending a small group at our church, and one evening her small group leader perceived something was off with her. Usually a bubbly and boisterous personality, her leader noticed how she grew still and seemed to be quietly self-reflecting. When the group was asked the question, "If you could ask God when you would die, would you ask Him?" her response was, "No, because I don't know if I would make it to heaven." She proceeded to tell the group, "I go to church. I pray. Yet, I feel as though there is this big wall between God and me. You guys talk about a relationship with God, but I don't think I have that."

After everyone went home for the evening, Lainey's small group leader texted her. "Hey, what's going on with you, friend?" Knowing this conversation required more than a few texts back and forth, her small group leader called her. Late into the night, they talked about the assurance of heaven and what salvation looked like. Before having attended our church, Lainey had never heard about consciously making a decision to choose Christ. To accept His death and resurrection and allow Him lordship over her life was nearly foreign to her. She grew up memorizing rote prayers and quoting Scripture, but she had never been shown how those Scriptures related to her own life. She knew Jesus was the Savior of the world, but she didn't see Him as *her* Savior. Coming to this realization, she knew what she needed to do. Her small group leader excitedly asked, "Are you ready for this? Are you ready to ask Jesus into your heart?" Together they prayed, enjoying such a sweet moment over the telephone. Lainey explained to me at lunch how she felt after they prayed. She said she felt chains come off her heart and drop to the ground–chains she didn't even know were there. Tears streamed down her face; her heart felt so free. Between our time together and her small group leader pouring into her, the body of Christ partnered together and led another sheep to the shepherd.

Can we pause for a moment to celebrate what Lainey's small group leader did through her group and their late-night conversation? Having people in our churches like her is exactly what we desire to have: disciples who are making disciples. Lainey didn't need her pastor to walk through the basics of salvation; she simply needed a believer who was one step ahead of her leading the way. What a gift to the Kingdom of God she is, as well as all the others who do the same.

I'm sure the restaurant's staff thought we were crazy as we laughed and cheered at her good news. This marked the beginning of her life as a follower of Jesus. She did not make this decision lightly. She knew this wasn't the end but that now God would ask her to step into a new season of growth. As she grew in her walk with the Lord, there were others to tell about her experience and how they can encounter it as well.

I'll be honest with you: when I say releasing a new believer to disciple someone else feels like it goes against our training. As pastors or ministry leaders, most of us were professionally trained in some way. Traditional college, church internships, or online courses brought us to the belief that we must know a lot before we can lead others. And yes, to lead a church or ministry, we need to know what we're doing. However, the only qualification to lead someone in the ways of Jesus is saying 'yes' to sharing about the freedom we've experienced with someone else. Together, we will grow. Together, we will learn how to live like Christ. And together, we will duplicate ourselves so the message can continue to spread.

As a result of Lainey's spiritual growth, both she and her husband are now learning what it looks like to live and love like Jesus. Her story continues to be written as she comes alongside other women to help them discover what she found in Christ. I remember her telling me, "I was talking with my friend the other day. As we were having our conversation, I noticed how she wanted to talk more about faith. With our lunch break coming to an end, I asked her if she wanted to have lunch again so we could talk more. And she did! But I'm scared, Sara. What if I don't know what to do? Or what if I say the wrong thing?"

It was like my orchestral days all over again. Could I release Lainey to disciple someone else, even though she was still so new in her walk with God? I wonder if the disciples felt the same way when Paul gave his allegiance to Jesus. Did they worry about him prematurely sharing the Gospel message? The book of Acts shows us how even in Damascus, days after his conversion, he was in the synagogues preaching about Jesus. Was it too soon? Could he be trusted to speak the truth?

Despite my initial pause with Lainey, the answer was yes! Later in his ministry, Paul himself said, "By his divine power, God has given us everything we need for living a godly life. We have received all of this by coming to know him, the one who called us to himself by means of His marvelous glory and excellence" (2 Peter 1:3). These words, which we've read earlier in the book, remind us how even the newest of believers have what they need to preach about Jesus to those around them. As Lainey came to know Him, the Holy Spirit dwelled within her. "He saved [her], not because of the righteous things [she] had done, but because of his mercy. He washed away [her] sins, giving [her] a new birth and new life through the Holy Spirit" (Titus 3:5). I had to trust the Holy Spirit poured Himself out on her the night she prayed over the phone. I had to trust I could keep Him at His word and give her everything she needed. I needed to be confident she was, indeed, a new person.

Undeterred by her fear, I told her she could do it. We looked back at her life over the previous year and were in awe of the growth we saw. There was still room to grow, but don't we all have space for that? She just needed to be one step ahead of her friend. Like the mighty Bur Oak tree, she needed to allow herself the freedom to multiply despite the newness of her faith. We continue to meet today, but instead of just reading Scripture and talking about her growth, we also talk about how her friend is growing too. While I could never fill my mentor's shoes, I became her Kami.

Watching someone grow as a result of our time poured into them will do two things: The first is it allows us to *celebrate their salvation with them*. Jesus said, "There is more joy in heaven over one lost sinner who repents and returns to God than over ninety-nine others who are righteous and haven't strayed away!" (Luke 15:7). We rejoice with heaven! Someone who has been searching–whether for life's purpose and meaning, or for peace in the midst of suffering–has found what they are looking for! Like the lost items we read about in the same chapter in Luke, they were once lost but now have been found. "There is joy [...] when even one sinner repents" (15:10).

The second thing resulting from witnessing someone's growth in the Lord is a *rejuvenation of our own faith*. Walking life with someone as they truly discover Christ for the first time will bring us back to our own memories of first discovering Him. We can relate with Paul when he said, "Yes, everything else is worthless when compared with the infinite value of knowing Christ Jesus my Lord. For His sake I have discarded everything else, counting it all as garbage, so that I could gain Christ and become one with Him. I no longer count on my own righteousness through obeying the law; rather, I become righteous through faith in Christ. For God's way of making us right with Himself depends on faith. I want to know Christ and experience the mighty power that raised Him from the dead" (Philippians 3:8-10).

Allowing others the privilege to experience the celebration of others' salvation and rejuvenation of their own spirit is a gift we can give them. In our church, our team does their best to allow active disciplers to be the primary spiritual parents in the lives of those they are investing in—even before the pastors are. We celebrate with them as they share about their friends who are saying yes to reading the Bible for the first time or are willing to let them pray over their families and circumstances. We cheer when their family member comes to a small group for the first time and when they begin to ask questions about faith and eternity. We jump for joy when their co-workers make the decision to follow Christ, and they ask to be water-baptized. We even commemorate with them as we allow them to be the ones who stand with their friends as they prepare to be water baptized—at the lake, in a pool, or in a baptismal tank on the stage during Sunday service. We allow them (not the pastors) the benefit of baptizing their friends and family in the name of the Father, the Son, and the Holy Spirit because it's not about the pastor leading others to Christ—it's about the body of believers leading others to Christ. We lead by example; then, we make room for others to duplicate the example.

Friends, don't be afraid to loosen the reins and allow your people the privilege to lead others in the ways of Jesus. If we are leading by example, we will find a slew of people in our churches who are ready and waiting to lead others. Let's not stop or delay them out of fear that they won't do it right. Instead, let's trust the Holy Spirit will lead them and unleash them to be disciples who make disciples.

Reflection Questions:

- When you spend time in God's word with someone, are they able to duplicate that time with someone else?

- Who do you see in your ministry who is more than ready to discover the joy of being a true disciple?

CHAPTER TEN

UNLEASHING DISCIPLES

"Don't copy the behavior and customs of this world, but let God transform you into a new person by changing the way you think." —Romans 12:2

It was a typical spring day in North Dakota. The temperature was cold, yet snow was melting under the warmth of the sun, leaving our roads wet and our cars muddy. I was heading into work after a rough morning of getting the kids up and ready for school. Quite frankly, I was crabby. That is until I saw a notification pop up on my phone.

As I walked into work, I clicked open the new message waiting for me and read the first line: "So my spirit has been restless and fired up to disciple." Did that just say what I thought it said? I was stunned. Stopping in my tracks, I found a seat and slowly read through the message again. Whoa. Is this really happening? Did they purposely message me about wanting to intentionally disciple someone else? I had discussions with others about inviting friends to church and small groups before, but up to this point, I had not yet chatted with someone about one-on-one discipleship. Talk about a mood shift.

My smile was brimming deliriously as I rose from my seat and nearly pranced to my desk.

The woman who wrote to me had only been attending our church with her family for about a year. In that time, I learned her story and how God showed Himself through the healing of both her body and mind. This wasn't just someone who grew up in church and knew raising up others in the ways of Jesus was the right thing to do. This was someone who lived through the hard stuff and, with Jesus, was able to come out on the other side. The first sentence in her message showed me two things: One, someone who was eager to talk about Jesus with others and wanted someone to walk alongside them as they worked through their nerves. And two, it was happening! Culture in our church was shifting to the point where we now had faithful attendees ready to be the church and not just attend one. I couldn't believe it. We were here!

Culture changing is not easy. Whether it's a church, a business, a school, a community, or even a family. Culture will not see movement overnight; it takes patience, time, and a whole lot of hard work. It requires a leader who is willing to dig down deep, maybe scrape a knee or two, and lead by example.

Kevin Oakes, CEO and co-founder of the Institute of Corporate Productivity (i4cp) said, "*Nobody ever transforms their culture. They don't completely change it. What they're really trying to do is renovate their culture.*

They're trying to get their culture ready for the future."[14]
The church isn't a corporate business, but isn't this what
we are trying to do in our churches? It's not that we want
to change the culture, but we want to bring it back to its
original intent of growing and sending out disciples–just
like the New Testament church did. We need to keep our
eyes on the future because we know that when we live
according to the Great Commission, not only are lives
changed, but the message continues to pass on from
generation to generation. May it not be said of us, like
it was said of the Israelites when Scripture says, "After
that generation died, another generation grew up who
did not acknowledge the Lord or remember the mighty
things He had done for Israel" (Judges 2:10). They had
reached the Promised Land, their leader Joshua died,
and everything God had done was taken to the grave by
the parents and grandparents who wandered the wilderness all those years. This cannot happen again. Culture
must shift back to the intent Christ had for His body of
believers: to live like Jesus so others may come to know
Him, to multiply ourselves and help grow His kingdom.

In his book *Culture Renovation*[15] Kevin talks about the
transformation of a little company we know to be called
Microsoft. At the turn of the century, Microsoft held a
monopoly on desktop computers running Windows,
Word, and Excel. "Microsoft Millionaire" was a term com-

---

14 Oaks, Kevin. "The key actions that transform cultures." YouTube, LinkedIn
Talent Solution, 14 October 2019, www.youtube.com/watch?v=_1RA3TOx-
OxQ
15 Oakes, Kevin. Culture Renovation: 18 Leadership Actions to Build an Un-
shakeable Company. McGraw Hill, 2021. Page 62.

monly used in the industry because of how quickly money would roll in for their employees. In business, they were at the top of the world! As successful as the company was, it became a surprise to everyone when Bill Gates handed over his CEO duties to Steve Ballmer in January of 2000. What once was a successful reign quickly lost its value as Microsoft's market cap dropped in half, washing away any "Microsoft Millionaire" dreams–all within Ballmer's first year as CEO. He learned that although he inherited the most valuable company in the world, Microsoft could no longer carry its monopoly as companies like Google and Apple gained momentum. It was clear they were in need of a renovation, but Ballmer was never able to get them there. For 14 years, although he oversaw the launch of successful counterparts like Xbox and Kinect, he also oversaw the decline of the company as a whole. Things weren't looking good. That is, until Satya Nadella showed up on the scene.

Having moved up the ranks in the company by 2014, he had been named the new CEO. Fairly unknown, he had both the tech know-how and the guts to push the limits and bring them back to an upswing. What was his strategy to once again bring success to this previously reigning company? Build something customers wanted. Unlike Ballmer, Nadella wasn't creating an environment of competition within the company where employees felt the pressure to perform. Instead, Nadella created a space for Microsoft's employees to collaborate–for the betterment of their customers. He said, "At Microsoft, we're aspiring to have a living, learning culture with a *growth mindset that allows us to learn from ourselves and our customers. These are the key attributes of the new culture [here]..."*

Microsoft's culture shift had to come from the top. Even if a few departments were finding success, the company as a whole depended on a leader who led by example. The same goes for the church. Even if we have departments or parachurch ministries that are showing success, if the leader(s) are not living out their calling as a follower of Christ, we will not be producing a multiplying culture. The church must multiply. If it is not multiplying, it is hoarding the Gospel, holding the best news within its four walls and peering through the windows as it watches the rest of the world suffer.

Aquila and Priscilla were great examples of people who carried a multiplying mindset. They had become good friends with Paul when he first came to Corinth. As tentmakers by trade, they helped plant many churches, which eventually landed them in Ephesus. Once there, Aquila and Priscilla decided to put down roots as Paul continued to travel and spread the Gospel throughout Asia Minor. As Paul continued on his travels, his friends established a church inside their very own home. Taking the time to meet with other believers, Aquila and Priscilla gave their lives to the call of making disciples. One day, as they were walking the streets of Ephesus, they heard a man speaking in the synagogue. This man, named Apollos, was found preaching about Jesus. They took note of his enthusiasm and boldness but noticed he was only aware of John's baptism. He knew Christ had fulfilled John's prophecies, but he didn't know the importance of Christ's death and resurrection. Knowing there was more for Apollos to learn, they pulled him aside and explained the way of God even more accurately. They not only wanted Apollos to experience salvation in Christ, they wanted him to be able to continue to spread the Good News wherever he went.

I imagine the culture within their home church was for people to be discipled and after a period of time, become a discipler themselves. There was no stagnancy allowed. For the sake of Christ, the message had to be spread. They not only would have taught this mindset within the four walls of their home, we see how they lived it on the streets. Like Apollos, we have many people in our community who know about Jesus, but they do not understand the significance of His death and resurrection. This was something we discovered time and time again in our community. I assume you have encountered it as well.

So what are we going to do about it? As leaders, we need to allow our knees to get scraped as we dig deep, make the time, and do the work. Our churches will reap the benefits of our obedience, and therefore, so will the hearts of all its new family members.

Terry Parkman is the founder of Next Generation Leader. It's a leadership group committed to seeing

NextGen leaders discover their purpose; they desire to see leaders empowered to step into the plan God has for them. Also serving on other ministry boards, and with the pastoral team at River Valley Church in Minnesota, he is an advocating voice for students and their Next-Gen leaders. I love his take on duplication. He is quoted saying, "*What the Western Church often calls discipleship isn't always discipleship, but celebrated relationships. We maximize the vehicle of discipleship (small groups) while minimizing the cost of discipleship (dying to self). The problem is [when] the numerical growth of a group takes precedence over its spiritual depth.*" I could've easily been satisfied with Lainey's growth, and just allowed her to continue going to her small group. I could've also been content with her inviting her friend to a small group to help it grow. After all, they're learning about the Gospel and how to follow Jesus, right? Regardless of such wins, the goal is not to grow the small group. Nor is the goal to fill butts in the seats of our worship centers and sanctuaries. The goal is for those attending to share the Gospel. Terry continues to say, "*We measure the success of our group based on the evangelism produced as a result. Discipleship breeds evangelism! The answer to the needs of [others] isn't going to be bigger events or more entertaining messages. The answer is discipling them deeply and **unleashing** them to usher in revival*" (emphasis my own).[16]

Unleashing followers of Jesus to disciple others looks like a variety of ways. In Lainey's case, it started with a

---

16 Parkman, Terry. Ministry carousel. Instagram, 10 May 2024, https://www.instagram.com/terryparkman.

curious person who was bold enough to approach someone and ask for guidance, which resulted in pouring over Scripture while sharing meals. For others, it may start with daily 10-minute conversations at the mailbox cluster, or weekly office hours at the coffee shop while chatting with the barista consistently. It can even look like standing next to another dad at weekend baseball tournaments and talking about the life lessons we teach our kids based on biblical principles and how those principles have changed our own lives too. As our friends and family grow in their understanding of Jesus, and His death and resurrection, and they eventually take the step toward a relationship with Him, it's go time. The process of unleashing begins then—not the following year, not after some training, and not after they feel smart enough to do so.

Growing up in central Minnesota, it was not foreign to see mushers and their dog sled teams practicing for races during the winter months. Watching them drive their teams around the lakes and trees was truly a beautiful sight. It wasn't until I was in my 30s I was given the opportunity to experience it firsthand. Dan and I were speaking at a conference in Fairbanks, Alaska, when we were given the chance to do a ride-along with some mushing teams. I was ecstatic!

As we walked up to the dogs with their owner, you could visibly see (and hear) their excitement. Even leashed to their stakes, they were jumping higher than I stood tall, yipping and howling with complete exhilaration. Preparing to get the dogs hooked up to the sled, the owner allowed us to help by unleashing the dogs from the kennels and bringing them over to the sled. While assisting, we had one instruction to follow: keep them on their two back legs. These dogs were anxious to get on the trail, and the second they would get on all four legs, they would bolt! And we saw evidence of that. Both Dan and I struggled to keep them on their back legs as they were anticipating another chance to dash toward the trail. Even without training, Siberian Huskies are made to run. With an instinctive desire to work, they require vigorous exercise and plenty of space to move their legs. What makes sled dogs so incredible is how they learn to run together in training. When unleashed, their robust energy gets turned into a collaborative goal they can meet together. Each dog plays a role on the team, depending on their skills and their temperaments. For example, wheel dogs (aka wheelers) are the ones closest to the sled. They need a calm temperament so they are not easily spooked by the sled behind them. Their strength and steadiness help guide the sled around tight curves, keeping it stable as they move along the trail.

When you and I are reborn in the spirit, we are, therefore, born to run. Whether we are the pastors, ministry leaders, lay leaders, or simply everyday attendees, together we run toward a collaborative goal: to share the Good News with as many people as we can. Our different skills, personalities, and temperaments all have something to offer to the team, and it can be easy to bypass new believers because they are still learning the play. That's the beauty of a team, though, because just like with the dogs, a new believer can team up with a seasoned one and learn the play while already running it. Let's not delay the process for them to run–they're ready to be unleashed.

I look back at where our church was when we first took the role of lead pastor. I often think to myself, "My how far we've come!" We have literally gone from people complaining about other's lifestyle choices, lack of morality, the new paint on the wall, the electric guitar in worship, and looking down on the poor and needy to people welcoming newcomers with phrases like "We are so glad you're here," "Tell me your story," and "Let's figure this out together." It is literally a night and day difference. I remember the shock I experienced in that annual business meeting all those years ago, and can now see the faithfulness of God as He began to turn the hearts of our own people. He began to open their eyes and help them see what stirs His own heart: people. Even when they are broken, immoral, or hurting, God loves them equally as much as He loves the upright.

Are we there yet? Have we reached the pinnacle of a multiplying church? No. But like Satya Nadella said, "*The practice of being 'vulnerable enough to say 'I'm not perfect, I'll never be perfect, but I can learn'–that's a good posture to have.*" I couldn't agree more.

So, what are we doing that has helped shift the unhealthy culture we once had? It started with us as the leaders. We chose to evaluate the heart attitude of the church as well as the condition of our own hearts. We set our pastor title to the side to first live as followers of Christ. We chose to be led by the Holy Spirit, take hold of the opportunities God put before us with the people we see often, and chose to be held accountable as we intentionally discipled others. Dan has sat across a lunch table from other men many times as they discussed the difference between religion and relationship. I've enjoyed early morning coffees with women as we've looked at the importance of seeing God's character woven all throughout Scripture. This was only the beginning. It has only continued from there.

Each of our staff members has one-on-ones where they meet with people inside and outside of the church. Whether they're at the gym, having coffee, or going for a walk, they talk about life, family, and all things faith with those around them. They allow space for asking questions like, "Why is Jesus so important?" "Who is the Holy Spirit?" and "What's my purpose on Earth?" Like us, they take the time to listen to their stories. Together, they laugh, cry, mourn, and celebrate. They do not spend this time with the intent of growing their volunteer staff but rather to show their world who Jesus is. We consider ourselves blessed to have a pastoral team that loves the people in our city (not just our church) so well.

In those one-on-ones, we begin to prepare them to become a discipler. We make sure all we do (reading Scripture, discussing questions, and inviting others to discover alongside us) can be duplicated while we balance the tightrope of patiently waiting until they're ready and gently prodding them to move forward. No stagnancy allowed. As a result of this, when someone comes to know Christ, we've begun to see people in our church start to produce fruit of their own. Here are a few examples:

Jessica decided she no longer wanted to be comfortable in her faith. An introvert by nature, she decided that it was high time she stepped out of her comfort zone and became intentional with the people around her. She meets with farm families who live down the road from her. They talk about chickens, gardens, and harvest. Once asked, "Why are you so nice to me?" she was able to respond with "Because I love you. And Jesus loves you too." She patiently loves and serves her neighbors, waiting for opportunities to share her piece in God's big story.

Andrew serves in the Air Force. Having moved up the ranks over the years, he has been given a position of influence, earning him the right for others to lend their ear. Although he walks cautiously, he continually prays for how he can be a light at every base he serves. Our community's Air Force base has been known as the base no one wants to go to, but he has taken that on as a challenge to show other airmen that while the landscape may be lacking, many who move here experience the power of God. While his job restricts him in some ways, he refuses to sit idly as people suffer from loneliness and depression. He knows he carries the remedy to their pain.

Hattie's relationship with God deepened in her 20s. Having grown up in the church, she never understood what a relationship with God looked like outside of traditions and rituals. Once she came to an understanding, her life was completely transformed. Not wanting a day to go by where she doesn't share the Good News, she chooses to disciple other women in what it looks like to be fruit-filled. Walking life with them, she hears their hearts cry for a Savior who will deliver them from their hurts and leads them to discover Jesus–who is so much more than a tradition or historical figure.

Matt was attending a church that had grown stagnant. Its leaders were not rising to the challenge of raising new disciples; he wanted more. Finding someone who would disciple him, he learned about the power of the Holy Spirit. He continued to take steps forward in his walk with God, which ultimately grew his desire for others to experience the same. He now chooses to spend time with students, pouring into them through their interests in both music and computers. Whether he's on a job or volunteering with youth, he duplicates what he saw through his own discipleship process in hopes of experiencing the life-changing power of Jesus Christ.

I could go on for pages and pages, but I'll just say this: when leaders lead, others follow. The healthy shift our church has made wasn't just because of what Dan and Sara did. No. It was made because of the Jessicas, Andrews, Hatties, and Matts, who were no longer satisfied sitting in a seat on Sunday morning, hearing a message, and moving on with their life. They saw their pastors and ministry leaders pouring into the lives of others, and they wanted to stand at the enemy line with them, side-by-side, declaring the enemy has no dominion over their community. They've taken on the mantle of multiplication.

Now, I understand there's no shortage of books out there on culture. It seems like everywhere you turn, there are leaders sharing ten-step processes on how to lead well, creating the culture you are seeking for your church or business. I'll admit I'm not an expert. I just know where our church was and where it is today. We've worked hard to live as followers of Jesus before living as leaders, and God has allowed us to see a new culture unfold before our eyes.

If I know you, like I think I do, you have a stronger desire to see people you are leading multiply over following some magic process. Because let's be real—there's no magic process. We know something needs to change, and we know it will take teaming up with the Holy Spirit to make it happen. Can you imagine what would happen if we unleashed our people? They're born to run!

How would your church look different if it carried a multiplying mindset? I may not know you personally, but as you've taken the time to read about our story, I consider you my friend. As my friend, I want to dream with you about what could be.

I see you. As you sit quietly on the edge of your bed, not quite ready to fall asleep, contemplating the day's events. Over lunch, you had met with a couple who were not feeling fed. Whether your messages are not to their liking or they lack a level of involvement, you know what the real culprit is. Even though your flesh wants to throw down the hammer and talk about the fruit of apathy you see in their life, you politely nod your head and listen to their complaints. Your heart hurts. Not because of an offense but because you wish so badly that they could see what they are missing.

I see you as you walk the aisles of your worship center. You pray fervently for your community as you're reminded of those who are fighting cancer, going through a divorce, or mourning the death of a child. You love these people. Deeply. As tears trickle down your face, you beg God for opportunities to talk about the hope of Christ with others. Their hurts surround you as you feel the weight of being a spiritual leader to the residents in your city.

I see you as you serve the next generation in your community. You work so hard to create events that will draw students in so they can hear the Gospel message. You intentionally build relationships with the schools and other organizations in town, all because you love students so much. Your heart breaks as you listen to their painful stories of brokenness.

I see you hiding in your office. The pressure to deliver a good message week after week can drain you. How many times will you preach on the life and teachings of Jesus before people will actually begin to live in response to what Jesus did for them on the cross? What if no one responds to the message? What if they all walk out the door unchanged? Your heart yearns for people to see the word of God as it is: alive and active. But sometimes the pressure is so strong.

I believe so much more for you, friend. I believe for lunches where people share with you how much the church has meant to them. They were once walking on a dead-end road when someone from your church saw them and showed them the way of Jesus. The love and care your church members had for them led them to discover the character of Jesus, and now they walk in hope and freedom!

I believe for disciples in your church who will go to the hurting in the community. They will cook meals, clean houses, and mow lawns for those currently suffering from illness or family turmoil. They live as the hands and feet of Jesus because they saw the example in you. I believe many in your community will come to know Christ because of simple deeds done by those who call themselves Christ followers.

I believe in restoration in the lives of addicts because the ministry you lead has walked with them on their journey. They will not only recognize God's role in their restoration, but they will share their story over and over again with those who have the same struggles. They will be a walking billboard for the love of Christ and His willingness to redeem.

I believe in Holy Spirit inspired messages that will challenge the body of believers to rise to their calling. I believe as God works inside you, it will pour into your congregation. I believe one day, you will look back and think, "My how far we've come!" Young, old, seasoned believers and new believers will thrive as they are led to live like Jesus. I believe you are the man or woman for the job and that God has called you to be a light not only in your community, but for your church that's ready to be revitalized.

Do you remember the story of the four lepers found in 2 Kings? There was a famine in the city, and they were starving. Desperate to fill their bellies, they willingly walked themselves to the Aramean camp in hopes to find food when turning themselves in. However, when they reached the edge of the camp, they discovered that it had been abandoned.

Having their cake and eating it too, they lined their pockets with silver and gold while stuffing their faces with any food they could find. When reality set in, they said to each other, "This is not right. This is a day of good news, and we aren't sharing it with anyone!" (2 Kings 7:9a). The good news was right in front of them, and although they initially kept it to themselves, they realized it was simply too good of news to not share.

Friends, I believe it can happen. Together, we can lead our people to the realization that what we have been doing is not right. I believe you will see a multiplying culture where your church develops disciples who make disciples. And I believe in a community that will be forever changed as a result of its people choosing not to hoard the Good News for themselves.

Reflection Questions:

- What do you see for your church and your community?

- After reading this book, what do you need to do to get there?